THE ART OF

CONNECTING

THE ART OF

CONNECTING

How to Overcome Differences, Build Rapport, and Communicate Effectively with Anyone

CLAIRE RAINES *and* LARA EWING

AMACOM

AMERICAN MANAGEMENT ASSOCIATION

New York · Atlanta · Brussels · Chicago · Mexico City
San Francisco · Shanghai · Tokyo · Toronto · Washington, D.C.

Special discounts on bulk quantities of AMACOM books are available to corporations, professional associations, and other organizations. For details, contact Special Sales Department, AMACOM, a division of American Management Association, 1601 Broadway, New York, NY 10019.
Tel.: 212-903-8316. Fax: 212-903-8083.
Website: www.amacombooks.org

This publication is designed to provide accurate and authoritative information in regard to the subject matter covered. It is sold with the understanding that the publisher is not engaged in rendering legal, accounting, or other professional service. If legal advice or other expert assistance is required, the services of a competent professional person should be sought.

Library of Congress Cataloging-in-Publication Data

Raines, Claire.
 The art of connecting : how to overcome differences, build rapport, and communicate effectively with anyone / Claire Raines and Lara Ewing.
  p.   cm.
 Includes bibliographical references (p.   ) and index.
 ISBN-10: 0-8144-0872-9 (hardcover)
 ISBN-13: 978-0-8144-0872-8
  1. Intercultural communication.   2. Interpersonal communication.
 3. Communication in management.   I. Ewing, Lara, 1954–   II. Title.

P94.6.R34   2006
302.2—dc22

                                                                    2005033223

Printing number

10   9   8   7   6   5   4

CONTENTS

ACKNOWLEDGMENTS

We are grateful to those who helped with this project. Our deepest thanks to those who participated in focus groups at La Agencia de Orcí, at the California State Automobile Association, and in Detroit; your stories and your wisdom made our ideas come alive. We hope we've told them accurately, at least in spirit.

Hector and Norma Orcí and Richard and Michele Steckel gave us some of their most precious resource—time—to offer insights into their mastery in connecting.

Our clients are our greatest source of energy and inspiration. We learn as much from you as you do from us.

Mentors kindly invite us to stand on their shoulders. Nathaniel Branden, Mark Clarke, Chuck Kelley, John Grinder, Judith De-Lozier, Nikki Moss, and Ila Warner may recognize some of their wisdom in these pages. We hope we got it right.

We couldn't get our work done without the continual support and advice of our editors, Phyllis Hunt, Robert Himber, and Allen Alderman. We're grateful to Adrienne Hickey at AMACOM for her insights and counsel.

Mary Holt, Leslie Jaffe, and Linda Williamson helped us with the story about Nikki Moss. Stevy Merrill added her insights to the answers in chapter 6, "Twenty Questions."

Family is where we first learn about connecting. Thanks to Ken and Mary Mick, Lara's parents, and to Robert, Allen, Dale, Shannon, and Caitlin for putting up with us.

Harold Brown is a fifty-five-year-old African American. On Tuesday, he will make a sales presentation to a team of IT guys at a hot new business. They're all white and young enough to be his sons. If they buy, he'll make his sales goal for the year. He knows there's more to sales than a good product and presentation, and he worries about how well he will connect with them. What they do in their free time, what music they listen to, or even how they make decisions are mysteries to him. He knows they survived the IT downturn—and survived it well—and that they have a reputation for a maverick approach, but he doesn't know exactly what that means. "How can I convince them I'm competent?" he asks himself. "Will they think I'm a dinosaur?"

David Smith, forty-eight, just bought his second bagel franchise. When he bought the first store fifteen years ago, all his employees were white, middle-class suburban kids. The staff he inherited at the second store looks entirely different. Two were born in Sudan; one is a lesbian Gen Xer with a nose ring; another is a sixty-five-year-old grandmother; and three are Latino. He doesn't know how to relate. They intimidate him. He's not even sure where Sudan is. And is it Sudan or *the* Sudan? Will it offend them if he says it wrong?

Ellen Russell is a thirty-two-year-old journalist who works for a Christian magazine. Later today, she will interview a well-known atheist activist in her city for an article she's writing. She's never even talked to an atheist before. "Where do I start?" she wonders.

As the global marketplace and e-business create greater intersection across cultures, time zones, races, and religions, each of us will increasingly be forced to connect through difference. Business results—a sale, the profitability of a small business, the success of an article—depend on the ability to communicate effectively across cultures. With this book, you can grow more adept at forging those essential connections. If you want to bridge the gap that separates people from different backgrounds—whether it's ethnic, perceptual, generational, gender, or cultural in nature—you will find a strategy here.

We have cast a wide net to collect specific approaches and tools from almost a hundred people in a variety of industries. They have paid off for other professionals, and you can use them right away. We chose three people—one of the three is actually a couple—who are masterful at connecting. We studied the way they interact with a wide variety of people. We learned about the principles that guide them. By observing their interactions, we isolated a set of steps they all use to forge strong connections.

We talked to groups in three cities about connecting through differences. Our goal was to meet with the broadest possible mix of people with regard to age, gender, ethnicity, sexual orientation, and country of origin. In Detroit, we held focus groups with Arab Americans, Asian Americans, Latinos, and new immigrants to the United States. In Los Angeles, La Agencia de Orcí, a Latino advertising agency, set up interviews for us with employees and clients. In San Francisco, the California State Automobile Association—AAA—arranged meetings for us with its employee resource (affinity) groups. In the focus groups, we asked every individual how she or he would like to be identified in terms of things like age, name, profession, race, ethnicity, and sexual orientation.

THE BUSINESS CASE FOR
CONNECTING ACROSS DIFFERENCES

PRICES: WHEN INTERACTIONS GO AWRY	PAYOFFS: WHEN WE CONNECT
Managers & salespeople fail to meet goals.	Teams collaborate to create better solutions.
Joint ventures end in lawsuits.	New alliances are formed and strengthened.
Markets close their doors.	New markets open.
Employers lose high-potential contributors.	Satisfied employees value their positions.
Teamwork dissolves in unconstructive conflict.	Teams develop efficient communication and synergy.
Executives miss market signals.	Executives tune in to trends while they are still weak signals.
Nonprofits fail to secure funding.	Donors understand and support the vision.
People pigeonhole others.	People erase stereotypes.
Everyone misses learning opportunities.	Everyone learns and becomes more masterful at connecting through difference.

When we wrote the stories that group members shared with us, we identified them according to their preferences.

Although our interviews and focus groups were held in the United States, we spoke with people who hail from more than fifty countries. Our consulting work has blessed us with the opportunity to connect with business clients and friends in twenty-seven countries on five continents. The ideas and strategies you'll find in this book work well anywhere.

What we learned in our interviews, focus groups, and interactions became the *Core Principles* and *Pathways to Connection* that you will read about here. We found that, even in the face of profound differences, there is always something that connects us. The insights and stories people shared with us add up to a treasure trove of useful skills and practical advice. We've captured it in a quick-reading format.

Chapter 1, "Masters of Connection," profiles our Masters of Connection and introduces you to the Titanium Rule—*Do unto others according to their druthers.* It's essential to all successful connections.

Chapter 2, "Core Principles," takes you through the beliefs that masterful connectors hold dear. You will be able to reflect on your own values and see how your beliefs and expectations affect your ability to connect. We found that most of the time, what you assume is what you get.

Chapter 3, "Pathways to Connection," takes you systematically through the process of connecting. Here you will find actionable ideas about how to clarify your intention, respond to subtle cues, detect biases, sharpen your perceptions, and gather useful information.

Chapter 4, "Points of View," shows you how to shift among three distinct perspectives. Great connections start with the mental flexibility to see and hear your situation from different points of view. Each change in perspective adds a new set of insights and allows you to create a holistic, balanced "take" on the relationship. The ability to shift points of view is a valuable and learnable skill that will help you consistently craft your communication for success.

Chapter 5, "Working with Differences in Groups," is filled with important information for leaders who work with diverse groups and facilitate meetings in other cultures.

Chapter 6, "Twenty Questions," poses frequently asked questions about connecting across difference and gives practical answers to challenges you may be facing.

Chapter 7, "Crossing the Bridge," gives you three compelling scenarios to analyze. Each gives you opportunities to apply the principles and pathways and to design methods for connecting with people from other cultures. You will be able to determine how different points of view offer insights and information that help you craft your own strategy.

Chapter 8, "Learning Activities," gives directions for facilitating seven workshop or team-building activities that help people close the diversity gap.

The "Assessment" at the back of the book offers you a quick appraisal of your level of effectiveness at bridging the gap with people who differ from you.

You can read the whole book in a couple of days. It's fast-paced; we've put the information into digestible chunks like charts and lists, and we've included lots of stories to make the ideas come alive. You can skim for helpful tips to prepare for an important meeting or business interaction.

What you won't find here are tips for connecting with people from a specific ethnic group or culture. We don't tell you, for example, not to show the bottom of your feet to Arabs. While that kind of advice may be helpful and certainly does come in handy when you have the opportunity to immerse yourself in another culture, we believe that the most universal way to connect is to think of each person as a unique culture. By paying close attention to what people tell and show you about themselves, you can learn to function effectively when your culture meets theirs.

We trust your copy of *The Art of Connecting* will become highlighted, marked-up, and dog-eared—one of your most useful possessions—for a while. Eventually, the strategies and skills will become so much a part of you that you will forget you didn't always do things this way.

MASTERS OF CONNECTION

Many of us struggle to connect with those who seem *different*. But there are a few rare individuals who are extraordinarily good at it. We were curious to discover what made some people especially effective, so we decided to study three such people to find out what makes them tick. We were certain that if we looked below the surface at interactions involving these masterful connectors, we would uncover patterns, beliefs, attitudes, and behaviors that could help anyone interested in connecting more effectively when there are differences.

Both of us listen to National Public Radio, and we pay special attention when Terry Gross interviews a diverse spectrum of people on her show *Fresh Air*. We decided to dig deeper into her success at connecting by learning everything we could about her. As we were thinking about people who connect particularly well, we stumbled across an article about Richard and Michele Steckel and their Milestones Project in the Denver magazine *5280* (that's the elevation in Denver!); that short article made it clear the Steckels had a lot to teach us—and that, in them, we could study two masters for the price of one. Finally, Lara has known and admired Héctor Orcí for nearly a dozen years and was curious to delve into his success at bridging the gap between diverse groups of people, especially the mainstream advertising community and the Latino market.

When it first dawned on us that the masters we'd chosen were all past fifty, we were disappointed. We had hoped our masters would represent both young and old. Then we realized that their mastery came from the lessons they had learned over their years of experience. They've interacted with all sorts of people through many kinds of difference in all kinds of scenarios. They've tried and failed. They've tried again and succeeded. They had talent as young communicators. And now they've been at it for years. It's all that experience that makes them masterful. Their beliefs have been challenged, and when those beliefs became obstacles to connecting, they took the time to examine their beliefs and change them as appropriate. They've experimented with certain behaviors over and over again. Over time, the ability to connect with all kinds of people has become an important part of each master's identity. Once we figured all that out, we knew it made sense for our masters to be older. Their profiles are rich with information about connecting with people who differ from us. If you're a younger master—or a master in the making—perhaps these stories will offer some shortcuts or encourage you to continue if you stumble on your own pathway to masterful connection. And if you are looking for mastery in younger models, take heart. We learned a lot from younger people, too, and you will find their insights in every chapter.

TERRY GROSS

We googled Terry Gross and got 1,670,000 hits. We scanned hundreds of those citations and then studied her book, interviews other journalists have conducted with her, and dozens of transcripts, articles, and print interviews to uncover the secrets to her success as a connector.

We learned that a typical day finds Terry in the recording studio, her elbows resting on the counter as she peers through her glasses and leans in toward the microphone as if to encourage it to say more. "I listen as hard as I can," she says. "I follow people into places they want to go and then lead them back."[1]

Terry has a remarkable ability to connect with all kinds of people, draw them out, get them to reflect on their experiences, and talk about themselves. She's the host of *Fresh Air*, a one-hour program distributed by National Public Radio to more than 450 stations daily. Since 1987, she has interviewed a wide array of people; they include an Islamic leader from Detroit, an Iranian filmmaker, a Chinese chef, a gay-rights activist, a former White House press secretary, an eighty-two-year-old rabbi, a conservative pundit, and a leading neurologist from the Harvard Medical School.

Terry Gross has an extraordinary following—nearly 4.5 million people tune in each week to listen to her in-depth conversations—yet she just looks like an ordinary person. She's tiny—only a fraction of an inch over five feet—and she often dresses all in black. Her straight light brown hair is cropped close to her head. She typically wears only a plain gold band on her left hand and a large watch on her right wrist. She often wears a leather bomber jacket she bought at Gap Kids to make herself look "reasonably hip."[2]

Her work environment isn't flashy, either. She sits in front of a microphone with a sign that reads WHYY-FM—the Philadelphia public radio station she works for—in a small, dark room with no windows. On the day she interviewed Ayesha Imam, a Nigerian women's rights activist and a Muslim, Nigeria had just withdrawn as host for the Miss World Pageant due to violent widespread protest from the Islamic community.

The night before, Terry had dragged home a bag full of tapes, books, and articles, and she had stayed up until midnight poring over information about her guest, the country she comes from, the political situation there, and events surrounding the pageant. Terry doesn't write out questions word for word; she says she doesn't want her guests to feel like they're being asked things off some random questionnaire. But she has a general sense of a set of questions that flows logically from one to the next, following a loose story line. She also has a clear intention of how she wants the conversation to feel and to flow. Sticking to her plan isn't critical; instead, she listens carefully, allowing the conversation to take its own direction, improvising if she gets an interesting opening.

The first question she asks Ms. Imam on air is, "When you first heard that the Miss World pageant was scheduled to be held in Nigeria, did you worry there would be problems?"[3] It's a masterful place to start. She's learned enough to know that Ms. Imam will be comfortable with the topic, the question will engage her, and she will be interested in talking about it. And Terry formulated a question that takes her guest back in memory to a specific moment in time. This strategy delivers an answer that is fresh and spontaneous.

The question reflects Terry's knowledge of the events surrounding the pageant—the Muslim protests against it, the riots that broke out, the conservative Islamic legal backlash—but Terry isn't trying to show off how well she's done her homework. Rather, she wants her guest to shine. Terry has based her question on Ms. Imam's preferences. She has stepped into her guest's shoes to see the interview from her perspective and then designed a question based on that perspective. She says that the more she cares about someone, the deeper she can take the interview.

Listeners would be surprised that Terry Gross and Ayesha Imam are not in the room together. Terry rarely meets personally with her guests. They're thousands of miles away—on the phone or in a sound studio—linked by satellite. While many of us might worry that geographic distance would exaggerate the gap between us and those we're trying to connect with, Terry prefers it. Although it might frustrate us to operate without visual cues to encourage us, Terry relishes being just a voice.

She loves the invisibility of radio. "Since we're not looking at each other," she says, "we're not judging each other by the clothes we're wearing or how our hair is that day."[4]

Since there are no withering looks and no one across the table to stare her down, it's easier for Terry to ask tough questions. Guests never see Terry yawning, checking her notes, or glancing at her watch.

Without visual cues, Terry needs to be all the better as a listener, tuning in to voice cues. Everything she and her interviewee need or want to communicate must be said in their voices. She gives guests the sense that there is plenty of time to converse thoughtfully with someone who is genuinely interested in what they have to say. As a result, her interviews often sound like two friends talking on the phone.

In response to the first question—whether she worried there might be trouble in Nigeria—Ms. Imam tells Terry she knew problems were likely to occur because both conservative Muslims and conservative Christians are uncomfortable with the idea of beauty pageants.

As the conversation continues, Terry doesn't shy away from serious issues—religion, rape, and morality. Her most pointed question—"Do you think that Islam is incompatible with women's rights?"[5]—might be offensive from another interviewer. But inherent in the tone of the question is Terry's acceptance of Ayesha's beliefs. Terry times it well, asks the question sensitively. And it follows logically from the conversation they've been having. Terry admits that, were she at a dinner party, she might not be quite so direct. On the radio, she cuts right to the heart of the matter, and she asks the tough questions up front. She tells Ayesha and all her guests to let her know if she is asking things that are too personal.

Ayesha answers unequivocally, "No. It's not what Islam is or isn't. It's what people make of it."[6] To illustrate, she tells a story that comes from the traditions of the life of the Prophet Mohammed. A young woman went to him and told him her father wanted to marry her to her cousin. The young woman wanted to know if her father had the right to do this.

Ayesha says the Prophet answered that he did not.

"Okay," the woman said, "I don't mind marrying him. I'm just glad to know I have the choice."

Terry pauses and waits an extra beat to make sure Ayesha is finished, not just taking a breath. That thoughtful pace gets her below the surface where she learns intriguing things about her guests. Imam tells her that, when she was twelve, she started a club for "good eating and good works."

"What was that about?" Terry asks, and it turns out that Ms. Imam went to boarding school, and the food was bad. And Ayesha was interested from the beginning in helping other people.

"So you got an early start there," Terry says, with the rich laugh that is her signature.

By the end of the interview, Terry has learned that Ayesha had an uncle who wrote about women's rights in the 1950s and that, when she studied in England, Imam felt fragmented by all her causes—women's rights, black people's rights, economic rights, and social justice. These details would likely have gone undiscovered by another interviewer.

In her interviews, Terry's goal is to connect people's lives and their work. She delves into their personal worlds—the people and events that shaped them—because it is the best way to better understand their work.

When Terry is interviewing someone, she tries to ask them about the cataclysmic moments in their lives—when they were in a car accident or struck by lightning—because those things change people. She feels that, if she doesn't ask about events like that, she misses out on important clues to who people really are.

She asks, "How did you feel?"—even though journalists are taught not to use words like "feel"—because the word helps her establish the work-life connection. For the same reason, she asks people about their failures, the mistakes they've made, the challenges they've faced. There's something in her tone that lets her guests know it's okay to have warts. "We're defined at least as much by our failures, the contradictions in our lives, as we are by our successes," she says.[7]

Interviewing combines Terry's love for reading, stories, and learning. Early in life, she decided she didn't have many stories of her own she wanted to tell but that she wanted to *hear* all the stories she could. "The whole world is filled with stories waiting to be told," she says.[8]

She credits her mother for her powerful listening skills. "She was a wonderful listener," Terry says. "I could have said anything to her. I mean the most boring thing in the whole world, and she was endlessly interested in what her children were doing. Maybe that helped teach me the importance of being listened to and the importance of listening to somebody."[9]

How Terry Gross Connects

- Putting the focus on the other person
- Being nearly invisible
- Listening
- Creating an atmosphere for unhurried conversation
- Researching
- Staying up-to-date with people, events, trends
- Respecting individuals
- Accepting different beliefs, values, lifestyles

When we analyze the way Terry connects with people, we are studying attitudes and skills she developed and polished over nearly thirty years. Terry is clearly a master at connecting. More than anything else, we believe her success is based on her attitude that *it's not about her; it's about her guests.* She's friendly, down-to-earth, and unpretentious. In her observer role, she seeks to be nearly invisible, putting the focus squarely on those she's interviewing. In 2004, Terry compiled a book of her interviews. In the introduction to *All I Did Was Ask,* she tells readers the question people ask most often about her is what she looks like. To answer, she tells readers about the jacket from Gap Kids—there's a label inside with her name in case another kid has one just like it. But after divulging only that one detail, she refers people to the book cover. It's black, and more than half of her is in shadow.

Terry creates an atmosphere that lets her guests know they have all the time in the world. Her skillful listening—her monitoring voice cues and pausing to encourage the speaker to say more and her love for a good story—tells them the focus is on *them.*

And then there's her meticulous research. Not only does she spend time reading about her guests—the countries they come from, the industries they work in, the projects they've done—but she keeps up with what's going on in the world. She subscribes to nine or ten newspapers and magazines to stay current on people and events.

Her respect for the people she's interviewing is evident not only from the time she takes to prepare to interview them but also from the way she treats them. Her questions, her tone of voice, and her hearty laugh demonstrate that she cares and empathizes. She doesn't pursue "gotcha" moments. "I respect someone's right to privacy, and I want them to know it," she says. "I feel that private citizens don't owe telling us about their dysfunctional families or their former cocaine habit. It's really none of our business."[10]

Some of Terry's favorite interviews were with Orville Schell, dean of journalism at the University of California at Berkeley. He was in China when President Clinton was visiting there, and each evening after a hectic day of presidential events, he would stretch out on the bed in his hotel room and call her. Then, he says, he'd turn out the light, lean back, and spend an hour telling her all that had happened that day. What Schell enjoyed most was the sense that he could think out loud and even try out some new ideas at a leisurely pace with a masterful listener who was sincerely curious about everything he had to say.[11]

RICHARD AND MICHELE STECKEL

It's an icy day in early winter, and Richard and Michele Steckel are bouncing along in a Land Rover that is winding its way up the side of a mountain in Lesotho, the tiny kingdom surrounded by South Africa. This is the Steckels' first visit to Lesotho, although they've been fascinated with the country for years, and they're hoping to spend the day taking photos for their Milestones Project. When the tour is over, they will have traveled to twenty-three countries over five years and taken 28,000 National Geographic–quality photos of the world's children—capturing their first haircuts, first steps, first birthdays, and other childhood milestones.

Richard is silver-haired, with soft brown eyes. He is dressed in wrinkled pants and a beige shirt, open at the neck. "The Milestones Project," he tells us, "is a nonprofit initiative that helps parents teach their children to value and respect people who are different from themselves." His soft voice is warm, resonant. "We're not professional photographers. We're picture-takers with a purpose."

The purpose is to help people see—one photograph at a time—that no matter where we live, how we pray, or what we wear, we are more alike than different. "We think it's harder to hate somebody who looks like you, who's going through the same experiences. Everybody's gorgeous and goofy when they lose a tooth," he tells us. He uses broad inclusive language—*empathy, hatred, violence, acceptance, promise, hope*—as he gestures with an open hand to his heart.

About halfway up the side of the mountain on one of the more jarring hairpin turns, one of the Land Rover's doors pops open. Michele grabs on to her seat, knuckles white, until the road levels off again. Then she and Richard fumble through their duffle bag, where they always keep a length of duct tape wrapped around a piece of cardboard. They tape the door closed. Michele eyes it warily, her classically beautiful face looking lived in, as if it has been used warmly over the decades. She has three daughters and seven grandchildren.

Once they arrive at the village, which sits atop the mountain at 11,000 feet, their young South African guide takes them to watch women making bread in a dark hut. They pat the loaves into shape, then bury them in hot coals to bake. After a while, Richard steps outside. Michele soon joins him. The panorama is awesome, and they scramble back to the Land Rover for their cameras. They perch on a rock and begin to snap photos of the broad vista below. Before long, Michele spots a boy in the distance running toward them. She can hear him singing and laughing, and she soon sees that he is sticking out his humongous tongue, flaunting it.

"You've got to take this," Michele tells him. "You've got the long lens." She's often the one who first spots a photo opportunity. The two work well together, signaling each other almost imperceptibly when it's time to move in, step back, or change perspective.

The photo of the boy with the huge tongue will become one of their personal favorites, the keystone of the "tongues section" in Milestones exhibits. It defies nationalism; this could be an exuberant child from any corner of the world.

The boy has approached out of curiosity about the Land Rover and the people who arrived in it. No one made an announcement that the Steckels were coming. They never do. Kids are drawn by their own fascination. They begin to appear out of nowhere. In Peru, Richard tells us, they came out of alleys and distant doorways; in Mexico, from around corners. They want to investigate. They hear something is going on, and they want to see what it's about.

Richard and Michele don't normally start by taking pictures; they usually interact with the children first. If adults are present, they ask permission to take photos. But the boy with the big tongue has warmed up the crowd, and by now there's a gathering of children.

"Occasionally, children are wary," says Michele. "In the beginning, they see us as strangers with cameras. But, in our minds, we look just like them. We are them. We're their age. We're part of their culture. We just melt in." To get the shots they want, Richard and Michele get down at eye level with the children. They bend on a knee or sit on the ground.

"Kids observe you carefully," says Richard. "They decide whether you're friendly, if you're to be trusted, if you're going to embarrass them. They're watchful."

There's at least one shy child in every crowd. At a Fijian church in New Zealand, a little girl about four years old arrived attached to the back of her mother's leg, stealing occasional peaks at the two strangers. Her older siblings were less reticent.

"It's okay," Michele told her with a soft smile. "Why don't you watch? If you want to join in later, you'll be welcome."

When they were nearly ready to leave, Richard approached the mother. The four-year-old listened gravely. "We'd love to send photos back to you," he told her. "Would you like us to get a picture of the whole family?"

Richard tells us the mother turned to the child, who looked up into her face with mournful eyes, then nodded her assent. The tiny four-year-old stood tall and proud for the family portrait.

In Lesotho, Richard asks a small group of boys if they'd like to jump over a rock. Even the shyest member of the group joins in with enthusiasm.

A couple of children speak English, so Michele asks them to make happy faces. Then sad. Then scary.

"A scary face is consistent all over the world," she says. "Another thing that's always the same is when we ask children to pose for us." Boys consistently pose as fighters or jump at each other. Girls get closer. They go cheek to cheek or put their arms around each other.

By the time Richard and Michele are ready to climb back into the Land Rover for the return trip down the mountain, they've taken more than a hundred photos. These are some of their best; the Lesotho photos show up disproportionately in Milestones exhibitions.

If you have an opportunity to see a Milestones exhibit, don't pass it up. The pictures are colorful, touching, funny, intense. "The photos remind people of our basic humanity," says Richard. The roots of the Milestones Project concept go back to Richard's doctoral studies at Boston University, where he studied the work of the Brazilian Paulo Freire. Freire taught that simple, repetitive images disarm people and open them up to talk about their assumptions, prejudices, and values.

Richard tells us about a time he and Michele were confronted by an upset man in front of one of their photos at an exhibit at the United Nations. "Where did you get this photo of my daughter?" the man demanded.

Richard explained he had taken the picture at the Johannesburg Zoo when they were in South Africa.

The man took a deep breath.

Then a huge smile crept across his face. "My daughter is from

Tanzania," he announced. "This child," he said, pointing at the photo, "from South Africa. She could be my child."

The Steckels find doing their work irresistible. For Michele's sixtieth birthday, they went to St. Lucia, in the West Indies, to relax and do nothing. By the afternoon of their second day, they were bored senseless, so they grabbed their cameras and drove to a remote school. By the time they were finished, their shirts were sopping wet and their hair was plastered to their heads from working in the heat. But this was closer to their idea of *fun* than sitting on the beach, and now they had a collection of striking photos of children against the rich orange wall of their school building.

"Our vision is to prompt 100,000,000 people globally in the next three years to reflect on, talk about, and take personal action to reduce prejudice, intolerance, and hatred."

Richard tells us that yes, of course, there are people who are cynical about the project—in which they've invested over $100,000 of their own money—but that skeptics are swayed once they have seen the photos or been involved in the project. A few years ago, the Steckels called a friend, Emmy Award–winning journalist and former CNN anchor Reynelda Muse.

"Would you help us evaluate our work?" they asked. "Look over our materials, our purpose, vision, and objectives, and tell us if you think we're on target. Come with us to Mexico. Ask 'why are you doing this?' and 'what's the purpose of that?' We want to make sure what we are doing isn't culturally biased. We need to know if it's original or if it's just more of the same old thing."

Reynelda invited Thandabantu Iverson, her husband, to join them. TB, as he's better known, is an African American who was involved in the social movement in the 1960s. At one point, he moved to Tanzania to live his life away from American racism. He apparently told her it sounded like "just another white guilt thing."

"Come along," she answered. "You decide."

In Querétaro, a little town north of Mexico City, the Steckels loaned Reynelda a Polaroid; they take it along so they can leave snapshots with the children they're photographing. TB wanted a camera, too, so Richard let him use his spare. When Thandabantu used up all the film in the camera he was using, he asked to borrow Michele's and directed her out of the way of his shot.

A couple of minutes later, Michele looked over and chuckled to find Reynelda taking a picture "up in someone's face," a practice she and Richard studiously avoid for fear of being intrusive.

A little later, in a crowded dentist's office, the two couples snapped photos of a mother and her sweet, moon-faced six-year-old. There are great shots of him having a tooth drilled, a filling put in, and his teeth cleaned. The mother hovered nearby, wincing as if she were in pain herself.

Afterward, Richard and Michele and Reynelda and TB piled into a Chevy Suburban to drive the child and his mother home. On the way, the mother gripped Michele's hand and would not let go. When the car pulled up in front of her house, she whispered to Michele, "There should be more people like you." Everyone got out to say goodbye. Looking around, Michele noticed there were no dry eyes.

"This passes all my tests," Thandabantu told them, his cheeks wet with tears.

The photos have been reproduced in a book, *The Milestones Project: Celebrating Childhood Around the World,* which has just gone into its second printing. The Smithsonian has recently scheduled an exhibition of the Milestones photos. Richard and Michele are now at work on a new photo project about grandparents and grandchildren. "When we can replace our fear of those who are different with a sense of our shared humanity," Richard says, "we will safeguard our planet from hatred and war."

How the Steckels Connect

- Having a clear purpose
- Being unobtrusive, focusing on others
- Responding to cues
- Building trust
- Relating to individuals
- Listening and remembering
- Using stories

Richard and Michele connect so well that they've won a prestigious award for it. In 2003, the United Nations presented them with the Global Peace and Tolerance Award. The foundation of their success is *purpose*. They have a clear set of goals—for their work and for themselves. The purpose of their life's work—to reduce prejudice, suspicion, and intolerance by helping people to recognize our shared humanity—gives them focus and energy because they have a sense that they are linked to something greater than themselves. They've even articulated their personal goals; they tell us, "We're simple people who want to collect mutually satisfying relationships and memorable meals."

Though their goal of touching 100,000,000 people in three years is immense, it's not about them. The spotlight is not on them; it's on the people and the connections. They're unassuming themselves; there's no slickness about them. They're soft-spoken and easy to be with. Especially when they're taking photos, they strive to be unobtrusive.

They believe so completely in their ability to blend in that they sometimes forget they're not eight years old, or Muslim, or Mexican. During their five-year tour, they were in Mexico in a famous park. Three hundred people were standing in a circle around a street performer. Richard and Michele were drawn in by the expressions on the faces of the crowd, who were laughing and looking delighted. They approached the circle slowly, Richard to one end, Michele to the other. The street performer looked over in Michele's direction and seemed to talk about her. Because they don't speak Spanish, neither was quite certain what it was all about. But it seemed good-natured. Everyone was laughing. When the entertainer was finished, Michele bowed. The crowd clapped and cheered.

Later, someone who spoke English asked Michele if she felt uncomfortable.

"No," she said. "But how did he notice me? I thought I blended in perfectly."

Richard and Michele know in their bones how to establish trust. When Richard was photographing a six-month old whose nose was three inches from a service dog's nose, he got down on the floor on his stomach. "I was totally unaware of what I was doing," he says. "My knees told me later that I'd been crawling around, but at the time, it was just right."

The trusting relationship between Richard and Michele says a lot, too. They work together like experienced hunting dogs who've worked the field together so often they just know what the other is doing, thinking. It's one other way they make themselves unobtrusive.

"Children know they can be wacky around us," Michele tells us, "and we won't embarrass them. Eventually we become wallpaper. They know we're there, but they ignore us."

We attended a meeting of the Consular Corps of Colorado with Richard and Michele. They were introducing the Milestones Project and looking for opportunities around the world to place exhibits in airports and other public places. It was an opportunity for us to observe them connecting across differences with adults.

As they showed their photos and told the group about their project, we noticed that they both are exceptionally responsive to cues. The way they listen—carefully, completely, making mental notes they can refer to later—makes everything else possible. Without it, they wouldn't be nearly so successful at responding to cues or individualizing their approach. They pay attention to details and then adapt their words and actions to match. In the meeting, we got an inkling of this when Richard adjusted the volume of his voice for a man sitting near him at the head of the table and when he moved into his conclusion because Michele alerted him that at least one of the participants was looking at his agenda.

Although this was a meeting of a group of people, Richard and Michele never approached them as such. They related to each person as an individual. They greeted the consuls one-on-one as they entered the room. Richard shared personalized stories that enhanced the photos because they related to specific countries represented at the table. He told the consul from Peru that they were so captivated by the scenery and the faces when they were in Peru that they took 2,400 pictures. "And when we were in Los Rosales," he told her, "people heard we were taking pictures at a birthday party, and the whole town showed up." By collecting and using stories, the Steckels show commonality and create rapport.

HÉCTOR ORCÍ

Héctor Orcí was just twenty-eight when he walked in and took a seat on the hard metal chair across the desk from Bill Eagleston in the executive offices of a well-known worldwide manufacturer of consumer products. Héctor and his wife, Norma, had just relocated from Chicago to Hato Rey, Puerto Rico. "It took me a few days to tune my ear to the lilt and timbre of the Spanish spoken there," Héctor says. "And the food took some adjusting. There was no salsa, no hot peppers. We had to make do with frozen tortillas."

It was Héctor's first assignment in his new job as account executive. He had no ad agency experience and none of the vocabulary that might make it seem like he knew what he was doing. Héctor, slim and sandy-haired, wore what the unwritten dress code called for—gray suit, white shirt, striped tie. He had shaved off his moustache because the screener for the new account executive job had told him, "If you keep that moustache, people will focus on it and not you."

Héctor had just taken a job with McCann Erickson, one of the world's largest advertising agencies, and his challenge that day was to save the account. This was McCann Erickson's largest client in Latin America. The offices were in a one-story concrete and steel building that was attached to the warehouse.

On top of Eagleston's big metal desk were lots of orderly piles of paper, along with a photo of Eagleston and a swordfish. Muscular, more than six feet tall, with salt-and-pepper hair, Bill Eagleston had earned a reputation in the advertising community for being a demanding client. He was unpleasant to people who set him off, with no patience for those who didn't do high-quality work delivered on time, on budget.

Talk about differences. Héctor was twenty-eight, and Bill Eagleston was forty-one. Héctor had only two years of work experience and a master's degree in economics; Bill was a veteran sales guy with an M.B.A. Héctor was born in Mexico, Bill in the United States. Héctor's native language was Spanish; Bill's was English. Héctor sat on the hot seat; Bill held total control.

"Bill was a rough, tough, gruff Yankee," Héctor tells us. "A very matter-of-fact guy. There was no way to misunderstand him. He was intolerant of people who didn't do things right. He only wanted to work with professionals."

Weeks before Héctor arrived, Eagleston had put McCann Erickson on six-month notice to terminate the contract. "In the ad business," Héctor says, "once you go on six-month notice, you're history. The decision has already been made."

"I decided to go see Eagleston immediately," he says.

He was scared witless. "But I had this belief that if I just shut up and listen and then say the right things, everything will turn out all right."

Héctor did have lots of experience with people who are intimidating. "My first two jobs," he says, "I worked in a demanding environment with tough, smart people. I had chutzpah and confidence."

He got a lot of those qualities growing up, as well. When Héctor was twelve, his father began working for the Mexican consulate. "From my perspective, lots of the ministers and cabinet people were intolerant older adults," he says, "but I had good relationships with them. I sat at their feet and learned—and I did it in both Spanish and English."

He also learned about how to deal with intimidation from spending time with his uncles. "I come from a family," says Héctor, "where as a young person you have no standing. Children should be seen and not heard, especially young men." But Héctor's uncles enjoyed being around him because he was interesting and a good conversationalist. He said things in unusual ways. He was smart, creative, insightful.

Once, when he was three, he was trying to climb a ladder outside the house. His babysitter came out and told him to get down.

"What do you care about this?" he asked her. "You're not the owner of this ladder." Instead of getting in trouble, Héctor earned his parents' praise for his creative thinking, and the story was told so many times it became part of family history. It's the first example Héctor can think of in which, by putting the right words together, he got himself out of a jam.

"Manipulating my environment and the people who control it

is what I've done most of my life," he says. It will come as no surprise that Héctor was often in trouble as a kid. He regularly had accidents that required stitches. One of his uncles was a doctor. The uncle not only sewed him up but also criticized Héctor relentlessly about being careless.

"I grew up being able to listen and explain things so I would get what I wanted," he says. When he was a freshman in high school, he was given a scholarship by the music department to attend the next year for free. Meanwhile, the disciplinary department was in the process of expelling him for bad behavior. All through his ninth-grade year, he rebelled against the priests and the upperclassmen. He ended the year with seventy-four demerits. To be reinstated, he would have to write the Declaration of Independence 148 times—twice for each demerit.

To Héctor, this seemed like an impossible task and a waste of time, so he intercepted the letter from the disciplinary department before his parents could get it. He had a plan. He told his parents he wanted to attend a different school, and he was prepared with information about the other school—its faculty, students, schedule, and offerings. He talked his folks into it and enrolled.

"We lived in Mexico, but I went across the border to school in San Diego. The school I chose was better, and I got a wonderful education there. Once again, I was able to manipulate things to my advantage."

All of this was preparation for Héctor's meeting that day in Eagleston's office. "I got right to the point," says Héctor. "I asked him what the problem was and why we were on probation. And I asked what he needed to see in order to take us off. Then I sat quietly and took notes."

As it turned out, there were some simple answers. The client had more than a dozen products—it was no longer just the company that made razor blades, and it wanted consumers in Puerto

Rico to know about its oral and skin care products, batteries, and appliances—and a complicated product structure: the target market for one product was young men; for another it was middle-aged women.

"As an agency, our primary role," Héctor says, "was to buy TV and radio advertising so consumers would know what products the client had and would buy them." Héctor learned that the agency was not delivering what Eagleston wanted—an easy-to-understand media plan that could be executed without mistakes. And he wanted to be sure his budget was being used wisely, that the agency wasn't wasting his money. "The problem was," says Héctor, "no one had been listening to him with the view of solving the problem."

"I solved it. Quickly." He stayed up night after night and designed a simple twelve-page plan that included Eagleston's ideas and addressed his concerns.

"Then I pioneered the thirty-second-plus-thirty-second piggyback commercial in Puerto Rico." In those days, all commercials were sixty seconds long. In the United States, agencies had just begun parceling two shorter commercials together, and market research showed the shorter ads were just as successful. Héctor proposed parceling the ads. This meant the client could get double the value from its media budget.

"Within six weeks, I had a letter on my desk taking us off probation and congratulating us on turning the situation around and renewing the contract. In that first meeting, all I really did was ask what we could do. Then, of course, I had to make sure we were doing it."

A couple of years later, Héctor had serious problems at home that tested the connection he'd built. Norma was going through a difficult pregnancy that required that she stay in bed. Héctor needed to go home and take care of the kids and the house.

"I explained it to Eagleston," he says, "and he was extraordinarily nice about it. He leaned over backwards to accommodate my situation."

In 1986, fifteen years after that difficult pregnancy, Héctor and Norma founded La Agencia de Orcí in Los Angeles. Over the next two decades, they opened up offices in Chicago and New York. La Agencia is dedicated to connecting the Latino consumer with brands, ideas, and innovations through advertising, public relations, and consulting. They've racked up an extensive client list, which includes names like Disneyland, Carnation, Pepsi, KFC, MoneyGram, MCI, and Verizon.

When we visited Norma at their home in Pacific Palisades one late spring afternoon, she told us about one of La Agencia's first clients, American Honda.

"They were wonderful to work with," she says. "At our first meeting, they told us there would be no quota of cars for us to sell." Instead, the company asked the Orcís to help it earn the right to market to Latinos.

"That first year," says Norma, "Honda did absolutely no brand advertising—no magazine ads, no TV commercials, nothing."

Instead, following the Orcí's recommendations, Honda did three important things. First, they supported the U.S. census drive. Héctor and Norma helped them design public service messages that showed Latinos why it was important that they be counted. Next, Honda sponsored the first U.S. tour of Ballet Folklórico de Mexico, which celebrates Mexican culture through dance. "Ballet Folklórico fills Latinos with pride," says Norma. "We videotaped people coming and going, and you could see it on their faces." And, since soccer is so popular among Hispanics, Honda sponsored World Cup Soccer.

These three efforts helped Honda build a bridge to the Latino market. The unanticipated result at the end of that first year was that Honda had sold a whole bunch more cars to Latinos. That year it went from the bottom of the list to number three. The next year, they rose to number one.

"Nobody expected this," says Norma. "Their budget was smaller than Toyota's." More than a decade later, Honda is still number one with the Latino consumer.

How Héctor Orcí Connects

- Being confident
- Listening intently
- Eliciting the criteria for success
- Putting the "right words" together
- Being creative
- Knowing two cultures
- Being responsive to the other party's needs

Héctor's entire career has been about connecting; the mission of his company is to connect the Latino consumer with products and ideas. And his own mastery of connecting with those who are different from him is what has made him so successful. He is recognized as a leader in the advertising industry and serves on the boards of the American Advertising Federation, the Association of Hispanic Advertising Agencies, and the New America Alliance.

He comes across with more chutzpah than our other masters. He is willing to be honest with himself, and he recognizes his personal strengths and weaknesses along with his unique qualities. He goes into business interactions with the belief that, if he does his job, the response is guaranteed.

"When I'm sitting in front of clients," he says, "they have as much stake in a good solution as I do. We both need a good outcome. Even if they're sitting there telling me I'm fired, it's something they would rather not do. I have an opportunity to turn it around and make something happen that will be good for all of us."

Héctor's chutzpah comes from knowing that by listening he can get what he needs to "put the right words together." In that meeting all those years ago, he saved the account by listening. As it turned out, no one had really done that until he showed up.

When Héctor asked Bill Eagleston what it would take to keep the account, he was searching for the criteria by which Eagleston would measure success. When Eagleston answered the question, the contract was back on track.

"As frightened as I was," Héctor says, "I kept telling myself to just shut up and listen. If I did, I could come up with the right things to say and do to keep the account."

Once he had listened, really listened, to Eagleston, Héctor was ready to "put the words together"—to come up with a simple, logical media plan and a creative solution to Eagleston's budget concerns.

Héctor and Norma are both bilingual and bicultural, and it's a key component to their success. "Norma and I have been transformed by living and breathing two cultures," says Héctor. "We can shift from one language to another, one culture to another. And we are passionate about building bridges between the two worlds."

THE TITANIUM RULE

The masters we've profiled here don't have one universal approach for connecting with those they differ from. Each has a unique style. Terry Gross spends hours—sometimes days—preparing. The Steckels speak in the universal language of photography. Héctor Orcí puts words together to solve problems in unique ways.

But all are masterful at what we call the Titanium Rule: *Do unto others according to their druthers.*

The Golden Rule—do unto others as you would have them do unto you—means that you treat others exactly the way you like to be treated. It works best when we're the same. When we're from similar backgrounds and have the same style and preferences, it's likely we can connect in virtually any setting, almost effortlessly. We can probably even make decisions for each other. If we follow the Golden Rule and we like sushi, we order sushi for you. If we enjoy big, loud parties, we throw one for you on your birthday. If we like to work through interpersonal conflict at the conference table with the whole team, we bring up our issues with you there.

But the Golden Rule can cause a disconnect when the other person is different. "Do not do unto others as you would that they should do unto you," said George Bernard Shaw. "Their tastes may not be the same."

Your preferences may not be the same as ours, especially if we're from different backgrounds. One of the first things La Agencia de Orcí does to serve client companies is to help them understand how the Latino market differs from the mainstream market.

Norma Orcí says, "Some of the worst marketing efforts have been hopeless and clumsy because companies weren't recognizing and adapting to the differences. I was once at a conference with almost all mainstream corporate types, giving a presentation and talking about how Latinos shop for groceries. We go daily. It's an outing. It's a social event to see the butcher and catch up on the latest news. Once a week, we make our big purchases."

A woman in the back of the room raised her hand. "Isn't there a way we can just get them to shop like us?" she asked.

"This was Golden Rule thinking," says Norma, "assuming everyone in the world sees the world as I do—or should."

Here's another way Golden Rule thinking plays out in business. Many people have become successful by developing dynamic speaking skills and by being outgoing. We've observed these usually successful people trying to connect with people from other cultures, continuing to do what has worked so well for them historically—backslapping, telling jokes, being the life of the party—even when they realize their usual approach isn't working. Then they repeat what they have been doing, with even greater enthusiasm. It's as if they'd studied a book called *The One Right Way to Connect With All People*.

"If that much boisterous enthusiasm didn't work," they seem to be saying to themselves, "then perhaps twice as much will." But when the person they are attempting to connect with comes from a culture that values the ability to quietly draw out the personalities of others, their efforts end in failure.

What makes Terry Gross, the Steckels, and the Orcís so successful at connecting is the way they tune in to individual preferences. Practicing the Titanium Rule requires two sets of behaviors. First, we get to know people as individuals so that we learn their *druthers,* or preferences. Are they naturally more straightforward or more diplomatic? More logical or emotional? Casual or formal? Leisurely or focused? Spontaneous or disciplined?

It's easy to learn to observe druthers. People broadcast them, and, if we're observant, we can find clues all around them in the environments they create. To learn their styles and preferences, pay attention to the words they choose. Watch their mannerisms. Notice how they're dressed. Check out what's displayed in their offices, how cluttered or neat things are. Listen—as Terry Gross does so well—to tone of voice, inflection, pace. Notice whether they take time to chat about the weather and ask about your vacation—or whether they get straight to the topic at hand. What do they seem to enjoy talking about? How do they approach projects? When they make decisions, are they consensual or independent?

How do they organize their schedules? Do they spend evenings and weekends at work, or are they out the door at five o'clock right on the nose? All this valuable information about druthers is available when you sharpen your observation skills.

Then, once you have some ideas—even just guesses—about the preferences of the people you're attempting to connect with, you can adjust your words, your style, your body language, the tone of your voice to match their druthers. If you're ordering for a friend, you order what your friend likes—whether it's sushi or a hamburger. You observe your friend's reaction when you talk about a big party you attended so that you know whether your friend would enjoy a large, raucous gathering or a quiet dinner party with just a few friends. If you notice your friend never orders a drink when you're out together, you offer nonalcoholic drinks as an option when your friend comes over for dinner. You observe your friend and listen to him or her and ask questions until you know whether your friend would prefer to wrangle with an issue that has come between you in front of the whole team—or whether your friend would prefer that you come to his or her office and close the door to talk about what's bothering you.

One of our favorite examples of the Titanium Rule in action comes from the only non-Mexican executive in a Latino TV network in New York City. While Court was attending business school, he met a woman from Shanghai. They enjoyed chatting with each other and became friends. One day, Court was sitting next to her in class, and she was slurping her coffee. Loudly, with gusto. It was driving him nuts. So he took a moment to focus his thinking on her, to think about her druthers, about what motivated and mattered to her.

He wrote her a note that said, "I'm not sure you're aware of this, but where I'm from, making noises with your mouth when drinking from a cup or glass is considered rude." (By the way, in

China slurping and smacking your lips are generally not considered bad manners—just signs that you're enjoying your beverage or meal.)

After class, she said, "Thank you for saying something. I want to be seen as a lady by my professors and fellow students. That information will help me." The way he tuned in to her druthers—that having good manners mattered to her—and then shaped his message based on them made all the difference.

The Titanium Rule is based on the concept that *people connect via similarities.* In this book, we're talking about connecting with people from whom we differ. The way to connect is to identify and increase our similarities. We can't change things like our birthplace, our skin color, or our ethnicity, but *we can find all sorts of ways that we're similar.* When we make the effort to match someone—his or her posture, gestures, eye contact, tone of voice, tempo, style, language patterns, expectations, values, or beliefs—it increases our similarities. Matching just one thing begins the process.

Practicing the Titanium Rule requires a shift in thinking. It requires empathy, awareness, and understanding. It involves finding ways, based on what we know about another person, to make stronger connections by adapting, experimenting, and changing the way we do things.

"It's not what you do or say," says Court. "If you always use the Golden Rule, you will make mistakes. You need to take the time to read the cues people give you and get the information you need about how they prefer to be treated."

THE CORE PRINCIPLES

Terry Gross is a radio journalist. Richard and Michele Steckel are grandparents who run a nonprofit foundation. Héctor Orcí is the

CEO of an advertising agency. They operate in different worlds. Terry rubs elbows—long-distance—with celebrities, musicians, and politicians. The Steckels connect face-to-face with children, parents, and grandparents of all colors and creeds. Héctor builds connections between his clients and the Latino market. Yet all four hold a common set of basic operating principles:

- *There's always a bridge.* They believe we can find common ground with all people, no matter how different they are from us. It's what the Steckels' Milestones Project is all about— reducing hatred by focusing on the similarities among children of many cultures at milestones in their lives. "I want people to look at these photos," says Richard, "and say, 'I get it. I'm just like that kid.'" Believing that it's always possible to find something in common will help you when you're tired or frustrated and struggling to make a connection.

- *Curiosity is key.* These four masters at connection are among the most inquisitive people we've ever known. Maybe that's why it took us a while to realize they were all past fifty; their curiosity makes them seem younger than their years. They're fascinated by people, especially those who come from different backgrounds. Terry Gross uses her curiosity as a tool. "One of the things that draws thoughtful guests to *Fresh Air*," says Orville Schell, "is the knowledge that Ms. Gross is among that ever smaller number of broadcasters who expresses genuine curiosity about everything."[12] Curiosity opens a mental door. As long as that door is open, there's no container for judgment and self-righteousness. It's impossible to be both curious and judgmental at the same time. "Curiosity is the universal resource state," says Héctor. "I'm constantly asking myself, 'Where is the bridge?' 'How can I use this information to my advantage?' 'How can I affect that behavior?'"

- *What you assume is what you get.* The masters approach each person they meet, no matter how they differ, expecting the best. They go into every interaction with anticipation and eagerness, asking themselves, "I wonder what I can learn from this person?" They presuppose that *this is a good person who has valuable contributions to make and important things to say.* These positive expectations contribute to successful outcomes. They make a practice of seeking out people who differ because they believe they can benefit and learn. By spending time with those who espouse radically different political and philosophical ideas, by hearing stories from people of other ethnic or economic backgrounds, by learning from those who are younger or older, they have enriched their own lives. "Knowing two cultures has benefited me," says Norma Orcí. "I get to choose between two very different options. There were things I didn't like about my own parents' parenting. Gringos have a more rational way of child rearing. They *think* about it. They read books about it. When I first came to the United States, I observed that my American friends had different relationships in their families. Everyone had responsibilities and took part in decision making. I took that and combined it with demonstrativeness, which is essential to Latino child rearing. I got to design my own parenting style based on the best of both. It's through differences that we learn about other options."

- *Each individual is a culture.* When Terry Gross is planning an interview with a Middle Eastern imam, she doesn't put him in a category—male Muslim from Iran, for example—and approach him with a set of rules for *how to relate to Middle Eastern males.* Instead, she thinks of him as a culture unto himself. Certainly, his faith and the country he comes from are important pieces of who he is, but Terry also pursues clues about his family, his beliefs, his education, key events in his life, his personal style, his artistic tastes, what kind of movies he likes, even the kind of tennis shoes he wears. Héctor tells us one of his mother's sayings was *"Cada cabeza es un mundo."* "It means *every head is a world*. She was saying we're all different, each of us a culture unto ourselves."

- *No strings attached.* The masters don't expect reciprocity. Terry Gross is a great listener, but she doesn't necessarily expect great listening from others. An interviewee may be promoting a book or an exhibition, but Terry doesn't expect that interviewee to promote her. Richard and Michele are friendly to everyone they meet, but they're not put off when others aren't as hospitable as they are. Most of the time, successful connectors are rewarded for their efforts and good intentions. "People have been generous of spirit all over the world," Richard Steckel says. But when people aren't receptive, these masters don't take it personally. They assume there's a good reason. Then they become curious all over again. They do their best to learn what caused the reaction they've gotten so they can be more successful in the future.

CHAPTER I AT A GLANCE

Here's what our masters of connection have to say about bridging the diversity gap:

- "The whole world is filled with stories waiting to be told."
  —Terry Gross
- "We think it's harder to hate somebody who looks like you, who's going through the same experiences. Everybody's gorgeous and goofy when they lose a tooth."—Richard Steckel
- "I had this belief that if I just shut up and listen and then say the right things, everything will turn out all right."
  —Héctor Orcí

THE CORE PRINCIPLES

Being effective at connecting with those from whom we differ requires far more of us than a set of skills. It requires that we hold a certain set of beliefs, expectations, and assumptions. We call these the *core principles*, and they include these points:

- There's always a bridge.
- Curiosity is key.
- What you assume is what you get.
- Each individual is a culture.
- No strings attached.

To illustrate, we've chosen a scenario that will show you how an experienced consultant with a great reputation lost his biggest client by violating all the core principles. As you read the following account, watch for examples of Jeffrey failing to • believe in a bridge • engage his curiosity • assume value • understand each individual as a culture • and attach no strings.

Garrett, the newly appointed EVP of global services for a well-known high-tech hardware and services provider, has worked in the IT world for as long as there's been an IT world. He is in Toronto midway through the second day of a challenging three-day meeting. He's white, in his late fifties, and powerfully built with a square neck. He wears a golf shirt—with no alligator—and khakis. What's left of his gray hair is cropped close to his head, and his rimless glasses sit high on his nose. He has been charged with integrating three geographically divided service organizations—Asia Pacific, Europe/Middle East/Africa, and the Americas—into one.

The events leading up to day two of the three-day meeting in Toronto revealed several red flags. Each of the three existing service organizations has its own charismatic leader, culture, values, and preferred technical processes. Garrett's new direct reports—those three charismatic leaders—have enjoyed ruling their own fiefdoms with little involvement from the corporate offices for nearly ten years. It will come as no surprise that the three are resisting this reorganization. But an extensive survey showed that customers want the same service no matter what part of the world they are in. So Garrett, in his first major action in his new role, has brought the eighty top service people from around the world to Toronto for three days to create a strategic plan for the integration.

He's the right man for this challenge. If he were the pilot of the plane you were on, you'd feel you were in good hands. He's calm and steady. He approaches every situation in a logical, linear fashion and in an orderly sequence. There's nothing flashy about him; his soft-spoken manner and attention to detail are the hallmarks of his leadership style. He's well aware that he's a geek. Everyone at the three-day meeting knows he plays golf with Bill Gates, but that's only because someone saw it on his calendar. Garrett doesn't drop names. In the past month, he worked behind the scenes to make certain there was a clear agenda for this meeting with well-defined objectives and a logical sequence of activities for achieving them.

Garrett arranged to have fifty customers interviewed. And he was committed to hearing from the people inside the organization about their perspectives on how to accomplish the reorganization, what requirements needed to be met to better serve customers, and what processes they felt they could integrate. So he also made arrangements for many of the service providers inside the company to be interviewed. Then he asked that the data be put on paper in a well-organized, highly detailed framework that could be used in the three-day meeting in Toronto. He wanted to make certain that the needs of customers and the people implementing the plan would match up and that the voices of both customers and leaders within the company would be heard throughout the meeting.

To help with this effort and to facilitate the Toronto meeting, Garrett went in search of an external consultant with a great track record and a strong reputation. That's how he found Jeffrey, who has a background in creativity consulting. An entertaining raconteur, Jeffrey had worked for dozens of large corporations running workshops in "out of the box" thinking. Jeffrey's process for strategic planning was the new hot ticket in other parts of Garrett's company.

"Perfect," Garrett said to himself. "This man knows our business and has a well-tested, systematic planning process we can rely on."

The big unknown to Garrett was that Jeffrey and he had significant differences. True, they are both white males born in the United States, but their styles are about as divergent as they can be. Jeffrey is persuasive; Garrett is analytical. Jeffrey is extroverted; Garrett is introverted. Jeffrey is animated and expansive, fun to be around. He has a loud laugh. Garrett is cautious, methodical, and restrained. Such differences can create powerful advantages, but when they're handled poorly, they can ruin everything.

Interestingly, one of the reasons Garrett chose Jeffrey is that Garrett knew himself—and his own style—well enough to know the group wouldn't find a process he was leading *fun*. He hired Jeffrey because he had heard that Jeffrey was entertaining and that the process he used was engaging. Garrett thought that if the

Toronto meeting were fun as well as productive, it would help the group to bond *across* their conflicts.

Jeffrey was looking forward to hanging out with Garrett, charming and entertaining him. He was a little late to his first meeting with Garrett a month and a half ago. He had been meeting with another group in Garrett's company across the parking lot where he had helped them devise a particularly ingenious solution to a problem that had plagued them for months. He was on a roll; his reputation inside this client's organization was improving with every meeting. He was feeling so good about it that there was a little swagger in his walk. Blond, with a deep tan, Jeffrey was wearing pleated slacks and a dress shirt, open at the neck, with the sleeves rolled up.

Within minutes of meeting, Jeffrey realized he didn't like Garrett as much as the other leaders he'd worked with here so far. Garrett wasn't as dynamic. And it was frustrating to Jeffrey when Garrett didn't pick up on the creative possibilities in his proposal to reorganize the group using a graphic facilitation process with colorful cartoon icons to post potential steps to integrating the three groups. Jeffrey had heard that Garrett was respected and well liked, but he was finding him dull and tiresome.

"It's obvious he hasn't attended any of my creativity sessions," Jeffrey thought to himself. But he bulldozed ahead. Thank goodness Jeffrey had something to look forward to and keep his energy up. He had just bought a river raft and a vehicle to tow it and was leaving on a white-water trip on the weekend.

Ten days ago, Garrett asked Jeffrey for a more detailed agenda for the three-day session in Toronto. Jeffrey thought fast: he had a lot to do to get ready for his raft trip, and getting the agenda to Garrett would take *hours*. Besides, he didn't like to be pinned down about his approach. A detailed agenda would limit his options to design on the fly during the Toronto meeting.

He decided to finesse it. "Let me walk through it with you

now," Jeffrey told Garrett. "We want the process to come as a surprise to the group. That will make it more fun for them."

He walked Garrett through one potential approach to the Toronto meeting, feeling impatient but resigned to the task. But Jeffrey knew, even as he was talking, that he would change the plan. He knew he'd get an even better idea right before the meeting. He would simply clear that with Garrett in the premeeting briefing in Toronto. He would call it "just-in-time planning."

Garrett had trouble following Jeffrey. He sensed Jeffrey's impatience. Garrett wanted to know exactly what would happen at each stage of the Toronto meeting so that he could prepare. He wanted to rehearse what he would say and do to assert his leadership every step of the way. He seemed to get a bit more detail each time he pressed for specifics, but Jeffrey gave slippery answers. Eventually, it started to seem pointless to try to pin him down. Garrett felt uneasy. Misgivings started to gnaw at his confidence in the outcome, but he decided to trust this guy's track record.

Now, in Toronto, the first day and a half of the meeting had actually gone quite well. But right before lunch on this second day, when it was time to identify a system for choosing which technical processes to use in the new integrated environment, turf battles came to a head. Garrett could see that, if they continued in the direction Jeffrey was headed, the territorial issues would get ugly.

As the group started into the restaurant for lunch, Jeffrey said to Garrett, "It looks like we need to redesign this afternoon's session so we can handle this issue without coming to blows."

Garrett's shoulders dropped an inch; he was relieved that Jeffrey had the foresight to see what was coming—and that he had a foolproof plan to prevent it. On the other hand, he didn't know what to expect. Redesign at this stage? How could he be fully prepared?

They sat down next to each other and ordered. Then Jeffrey began to throw ideas out. He gestured expansively. He raised his voice. He began to talk faster and faster. He was in his element, his creative fires burning. Everyone in the group—except for Garrett—was eating it up. They were enjoying Jeffrey's creative approach, laughing at the hilarious stories he was telling.

Garrett's eyes began to glaze over. He shifted from side to side in his chair. But Jeffrey didn't notice. He was too busy being the life of the party. Engrossed in his own creative process, he forgot that Garrett's druthers were for a steady, systematic approach. Jeffrey assumed Garrett understood that Jeffrey was modeling a session of creative brainstorming and that they would soon start to narrow the ideas down to a few and choose one or two to implement. But Garrett was overwhelmed by the forty-nine ideas Jeffrey had flung out in no particular order. By the end of lunch, Garrett was exhausted and frustrated. What's worse, nothing had been decided.

The afternoon session was delayed by an hour and a half. Eighty senior executives scattered around the building to crunch through their e-mail, deliver orders to subordinates on their cell phones, and visit with each other about their investment strategies and vacation plans. In the conference room, Jeffrey and a few others finally calmed Garrett enough to reconvene the meeting. The group limped through the afternoon and the next day. But the minute the Toronto meeting ended, the relationship was over, the connection broken. Jeffrey never worked for Garrett's company again.

What a mess. We think the way Jeffrey violated the Titanium Rule should be a prosecutable offense! He followed the Golden Rule, indulging his own druthers: he treated Garrett exactly the way he himself likes to be treated—creatively, energetically, spontaneously. Since Jeffrey was the paid consultant, he needed to pay attention to Garrett's style and preferences and then *adapt his style to match*.

There were clues galore about Garrett's druthers. As a matter of fact, they were the very things that Jeffrey didn't like about Garrett—his linear, logical, analytical approach. Jeffrey needed to change his style when he was working with Garrett, to slow down and talk Garrett through a sequential process. He needed to come up with a logical plan and then help Garrett understand each step in it. He needed to talk through with Garrett how each part would play out. Jeffrey is a big-picture guy, a visionary; Garrett is a detail guy who wants things broken down into smaller, more manageable bits. Jeffrey was too busy being brilliant to adapt to their differences. He was counting on his charm to get him through. After all, it had earned him great success in every part of the organization he'd worked with so far. Had he stopped for a deep breath and taken an inventory of what was going on around him—at that first planning session or even in the three-day meeting—he might have seen the simple solution: to adapt his own style.

That's not the only place Jeffrey went wrong. In all kinds of ways, his actions weren't consistent with the beliefs and expectations—*the core principles*—that lead to success at connecting with those we differ from.

THERE'S ALWAYS A BRIDGE

Those who connect successfully in the face of difference have a fundamental belief in commonality. They assume that there's always *something* we have in common. While others walk away, polarized, and give up on making a connection, masterful connectors hang in there because they believe that, if they just persevere, they can certainly find common ground. Jeffrey didn't seem to hold this belief. He noticed all the ways he and Garrett were different; he failed to notice what they had in common.

Imagine that, when he noticed he didn't like Garrett as much as the other leaders he'd met—and that happened almost immediately—he had asked himself, "Okay, where's the bridge here?" or "What's going on with *me?* I'm not usually so judgmental, especially of clients. My reaction won't help me make this work."

He would have realized that he and Garrett agreed on a few significant points. They shared a belief that giving people a say in the process would drive better decisions and attain greater buy-in. And they both wanted a successful outcome for the three-day meeting in Toronto. In the planning meeting, Jeffrey and Garrett could have talked through and written down the outcomes they wanted—to get buy-in for the reorganization, to kick it off in a positive way, to let people know that all three existing organizations would be heard, to provide a forum for merging processes. What a great way that would have been to connect and get started.

In business, we're often thrown in with people with whom we seem incompatible. It's something we have little control over, and it can seem to us that we have absolutely nothing in common. It may be that your values and beliefs differ radically from your colleague's—and that your colleague's beliefs are those you've spent a lifetime fighting against. Or he chews tobacco and you're a health nut. Or she grew up in Mauritius and you're wondering, "Where in the world is Mauritius?"

But no matter how different we seem to be, there's always an inroad. If we step back and ask ourselves, "Where's the bridge in this scenario?"—knowing with certainty there is one—we can *always* find one. It may be that we both want to make certain the project is completed on time. Or maybe we both want our efforts to be recognized. Or we both want to get through the afternoon without a headache. There's always something, even if it's only that we both root for the same football team or enjoy the same kind of coffee or watch *The West Wing.*

When we're different and we focus on our differences, it's easy to forget that we're all human—that there are experiences we've all been through, feelings we've all had. It's those universal human experiences that Richard and Michele Steckel depict in their photographs, in hopes that people will look at the photos and feel a sense of commonality instead of judging and labeling those who differ from them. A child losing a tooth in Lima, Beijing, or Rome is exactly that—a child losing a tooth.

The Steckels tell us about a time a colleague was in the Miami Airport during a security breach. She approached a security worker whose name tag said he was from Ethiopia and asked if he knew where the Milestones photos were displayed in the airport.

He said, "You mean the teeth. I'll take you."

By the time they reached the exhibit, three or four other employees had joined them. People weren't getting through the tedious security lines, but one of their group approached the screeners at the X-ray counter and told them, "These are the people with the teeth."

They waved them through. The universal experience of losing a tooth had created a bridge, one that broached racial differences—and that led the traveler through security on that particular day.

Offers

In human interactions, people regularly put forward a piece of information about themselves in hopes of finding a bridge. We call this an *offer*. Sometimes offers are accepted; sometimes they're blocked.

Our friend Doris is an American who doesn't speak French. A few years ago, she unknowingly ended up in the wrong kind of hotel in Paris. Around midnight, a man—whom she thought looked like he might be American—entered her room with a key and said something to her in French. Apparently, he believed he had paid downstairs for her services.

"What are you doing in here?" she yelled at him. "I'm from Wyoming!"

"I'm from Ohio!" he yelled back.

"My husband is from Ohio!" she yelled in response.

They went on to talk about *where* in Ohio while she found her bathrobe. Then together they went down to the main desk where the misunderstanding was straightened out and Doris got a special key that would lock her door from the *inside*.

When she shouted to the intruder that she was from Wyoming, she was making an offer. She suddenly found herself in a scary and awkward situation, and her first response was to search for common ground. It worked. When he yelled that he was from Ohio, he was making a counteroffer, one that she accepted when she responded that her husband was from Ohio, too. As bizarre as the situation was, she clung to her belief that there was a bridge there somewhere, and her quick thinking produced an offer.

Norma Orcí tells about being new to Los Angeles and making offers when she encountered people she didn't know yet.

She told an Anglo coworker, "We just moved here from Mexico City."

"Oh, that's nice," her colleague said. "Did you see *Cheers* last night?"

Norma was making an offer, revealing something important about herself. By ignoring what she said and changing the subject, the coworker blocked the offer.

In improvisational theater, actors together create a coherent scene without rehearsal. The glue that binds the performance comes from each actor's accepting what he or she is offered. For example, if the troupe is asked to dramatize part of the Cinderella story and one actor takes off his shoe, goes down on one knee, and holds it out to another, he is making an offer. He is asking through his actions, "Would you like to play the part of Cinderella?" If the other actor accepts the shoe, it means he has accepted the role. If not, he has blocked the offer.

The basic principle in improv is called "Yes, and . . . " It means accepting offers and building on them. Jamar, a Denver doctor, has taken writing workshops and seminars for the past two years. He has a full-time medical practice and doesn't really consider himself a writer, but he is working on a novel. He's written nine pages. Recently, he went to a fundraiser and was seated next to Chris Offutt, an award-winning author.

"So you're a writer," Chris said to Jamar by way of greeting. It was an offer, but Jamar wanted Chris to know he didn't consider himself in the same league.

"Oh, no. I'm just a dabbler," Jamar said.

"I'm just a dabbler who persisted," Chris answered, accepting *Jamar's* offer and building on it.

When Norma offered the information about her move, she was inviting her coworker to connect with her. She was pointing out a possible bridge. Her colleague blocked the offer. It's possible she knew almost nothing about Mexico City and felt ignorant, that she didn't know where to go with the offer, didn't know how to accept it, and didn't know how to add an *and* to it.

When we believe there's always a bridge, we search harder for the *Yes, and* . . . . We know we can go to those universal human experiences to find one. In Norma's story, the coworker could have looked back on times she had gone through major changes herself to find aspects she might have shared with Norma.

Reflecting on it today, Norma suggests a couple of questions that would have validated rather than invalidated her offer. Her colleague could have asked, "How has the transition been for you?" or "How do you organize a move across an international border?"

In the coworker's defense, her intention was probably positive.

She was trying to find a similarity. Drawing a blank on the move from Mexico City, she went to another option. The table below gives examples of offers.

OFFER	BLOCKED	ACCEPTED	BUILDING ON THE OFFER
"Everything I look up in this manual just confuses me more."	"Are you going out for coffee this morning?" "I've got a new laptop."	"Last week, I read a whole chapter and knew even less when I was finished."	"I know what you mean. Have you tried this one? It seems clearer to me."
"I've decided to start my own consulting business."	"I'm thinking of retiring at the end of this fiscal year." "What's the stock market doing this morning?"	"That's great." "Good for you. You've certainly got the talent." "That's amazing. I was just telling Li how good you'd be at something like that."	"I can't wait to start sending you clients." "Will you have offices here in Atlanta?"
"I'm working on a new policy manual."	"I'm working on the annual report."	"It's about time." "That should be interesting."	"Is there any way I can help?" "Which part do you think will be most challenging?"

Persistence

Roger Fisher, the well-known negotiations expert from the Harvard Law School, reminds us that the most basic strategy for building long-term relationships is to be unconditionally constructive. That means that, no matter what others do, you're constructive. If they slap you in the face, you're constructive.

You might turn the other cheek. Or you might ask, "How did I offend you? Do you mind telling me what I did?"

Being unconditionally constructive means always keeping in mind where you're trying to take the interaction. Instead of judging or feeling self-righteous or trying to decide who is right and who is wrong or who's to blame, you stay focused on the outcome you want.

Ana, who is twenty-four and works in Chicago, tells us about trying to find a way to connect with her client who worked for Allstate. After speaking to each other briefly on the phone, the two met face-to-face for the first time at a luncheon presentation. Ana tried like crazy all through lunch to find common ground. Her client was obviously trying to do the same thing.

Over salad, each of them made quick statements, throwing out offers, but each one was blocked. Ana was born in Colombia; her client was born in Columbus. The client was older and plain— jeans, tennis shoes, no makeup; Ana dresses expressively and wears bright dresses and interesting jewelry. One mentioned a favorite restaurant; the other had never heard of it. One talked about a movie she especially enjoyed; the other said she didn't like that kind of movie. One even went out of her way to praise the dessert; the other said she thought it was awful. They fumbled and mumbled and seemed to have nothing in common.

"What will I do?" Ana wondered. She needed a way to connect with her client. Believing *there's always a bridge,* she tried another *offer*.

"What did you do in the past for Allstate?" she asked. It turned out her client had worked with computers creating pictures and doing graphics. She said she was really into her Macintosh. Ana didn't know a thing about Macs, but the last thing she was going to do was block this offer.

As luck would have it, she had just read about the iPod Shuffle.

"So we had a really good time talking about iPods," Ana tells us. "When it was time to say goodbye, I said, 'Let me see where you sit so I'll know where to find you next time I'm here.' She showed me her iPod, her speakers, her playlist, everything. She told me when I got mine I should come in and she'd show me how to download music. She said she'd do it for me. Now we talk on the phone and catch up on whether I've been to the Apple store and what new accessories I've got."

Believing there's always a bridge gives you persistence. When you know it's not *if you can* connect, it's *what* you can connect *about*, you don't give up. Even when you've tried and failed to find common ground with an officemate, or you've fumbled through trying to develop rapport with a potential client, or you've struggled to find something to like about someone who reports to you, this belief encourages you to hang in there and extend offers, knowing eventually you'll find one that builds the bridge.

"People are people," says Sal, who lives in Detroit and was born in the Middle East. "They want to raise their kids. They want to be treated fairly. They want people to smile at them." Sal is right. No matter how great the cultural gap, a genuine smile means the same thing everywhere in the world. It always translates as an offer. And a smile actually triggers positive emotions in your body. The social psychologist Robert Zajonc found that when we contract our facial muscles into a smile, we alter the blood flow to the brain and end up feeling happier. A smile will affect your assumptions and expectations.

CURIOSITY IS KEY

Curiosity is the universally resourceful state of mind. When we're curious, it's almost impossible to be depressed, afraid, angry, judgmental, or intolerant. There's an inherent friendliness in curiosity, an oddly optimistic frame of mind. Because our attention is directed *outward,* curiosity sets us up to be successful in connecting with others.

Jeffrey, in his interactions with Garrett and Garrett's division, didn't seem to believe that *curiosity is key*. If curiosity were a deeply held value for Jeffrey, he would have known the moment he began judging Garrett—as dull and plodding—that he had closed a trap door on his curiosity. Jeffrey was wrapped up in himself. Had he remained open and curious, he would have been eager to learn about Garrett and his organization, to learn everything he could about Garrett's world.

Curiosity has gotten Richard Steckel through some tight jams and hairy situations. When he was in his twenties, he was an activist working for the Unitarian Universalist Service Committee. He smuggled money to save starving people in Biafra and to get dissidents out of South Africa.

"When others get scared," he says, "I get curious."

His courage was tested on the trip in the Land Rover up to the high-mountain village in Lesotho. The road was slippery and wet; rain was pouring down, and around every hairpin turn was a spot where most of the road had washed away, leaving gaping holes the vehicle might plunge through at any time. But Richard sat at the window, fascinated by all the trucks and other vehicles that had gone over the edge. He counted them.

In Guinea-Bissau, on the west coast of Africa, he was arrested during a coup. There were bodies hanging from the bridges. Cuban soldiers with big weapons patrolled the streets. Richard had the same reaction in both situations: curiosity won over fear. Held in detention and awaiting deportation, he said to himself, "I'm getting out of here tomorrow, but I'm here now. I'll probably never be here again, so I'm going to pay attention and observe all I can. I may never have another experience like this."

We noticed this trait in each of our masters. It shows up in different ways.

Terry Gross is known for her inquisitive nature. No matter the subject, she's fascinated by it. She soaks up information, reading extensively, listening to tapes, and watching video clips at home in preparation for each radio interview. The process of "mining" for information helps her connect with her guests on a deeper level so that she can elicit stories they've never told before and understand the significance of their experiences to them.

Curiosity is good for you. The staff of *Psychology Today* reports that curiosity is one of the top five qualities of people who are most satisfied in life.[1] The North Central Regional Educational Laboratory reports that students who are curious tend to learn more, find patterns, and test hypotheses. They're more up-to-date on current events. They handle change better, react positively when unusual things happen, and are attracted to new people and experiences. When we're curious, we are stimulating our brains, keeping our minds sharper as we age.[2]

After September 11, Arab Americans found that people became more curious about them. Says Fouad, a marketing professional who was born in Lebanon, "Since 9/11, lots of people have approached me. They're curious. They seem open-minded. Their questions seem to be from the heart. They ask, 'Where are you from? What do you do? What's it like in the Middle East?' They want to know about Afghanistan and Iraq. I think people hear things in the news and they want help to know what's correct and realistic. The news doesn't give the full picture, so people want to know more about the actual situation. Especially about religion."

But curiosity has a shadow side. We learned a lot about that from a man whose differences are hard to ignore. Ron Bachman was born without a sacrum or lumbar spine. When he was an infant, his legs and feet were held in place only by his skin and actually got in his way when he tried to stand or walk. When he was four years old, doctors amputated his legs so that he could be more mobile. He gets around very well today using his arms and hands. Ron is forty-seven now, living in Detroit, and has made the most of his difference. He teaches tolerance and acceptance in schools and corporations.

"Curiosity is good as long as it's respectful," Ron tells us. "When someone asks me questions and I can tell they're trying to connect with me, that's great. It's not okay when someone stops me in the grocery store and asks, 'Oh my God, what happened to you?' Here's another thing that bothers me: I don't like people trying to figure out what body parts I have and don't have. Like everyone, I'm sensitive. Don't ask me how I go to the bathroom. Those questions create a barrier between us. You don't need to know the answer to everything."

Ron says he typically gets questions about his anatomy ten or eleven times a day. If you were to meet him for the first time today, you might stop and think about what his druthers would likely be. You might realize that he faces questions about his disability day in and day out, so a wise first offer would be one that emphasizes similarities instead of differences. It might be something like, "How about those Lions?"

Curiosity leads to flexibility, which is essential not only for connecting but for survival in today's complex and changing business environment. There's an old adage that if I've got only one choice in a situation, I'm a robot. With two choices, I've got a dilemma. It's when I have three or more choices that I gain autonomy and flexibility. Carl Sagan said that a passion for discovery is hardwired into all human beings. Thousands of years ago, when a cavewoman heard a noise in the bush at the edge of her cave, she was curious. She went and checked it out to make certain it wasn't a threat. Today, if we get a whiff of something burning, it arouses our curiosity and we check it out. Or, when we get a hint that there's a hot new business trend waiting to be uncovered, we explore it. Or when people who seem new and different come along, we seek them out for their fresh perspectives.

We were friends and admirers of Jean Yancey, who inspired thousands of women entrepreneurs. Jean was recognized with dozens of awards; in 1982, she was honored at the White House as Advocate of the Year to Women in Small Business. In Denver, she was known as the mother of all businesswomen. Jean died in

2000 at the age of eighty-six. She was confined to a wheelchair for her last few years, but age, pain, and illness never interfered with her curiosity. Jean was fascinated by the millennium; she spent the final year of her life reading about the first millennium so she could understand the importance of the one she was living through and discover the parallels between them.

In neurological terms, the greatest advantage of curiosity is the increase in connections inside the brain. "Investigating the unusual creates new neurological pathways," says Washington State University professor Richard Taflinger. "The more pathways, the more possible responses to stimuli; the more possible responses, the greater likelihood of a proper response to another novel situation. Curiosity strengthens these learned responses."[3]

This was an essential theme—connecting with people and cultures that are different gives us more choices and makes us more flexible—that emerged from our interviews and focus groups. Rose, a first-generation immigrant of Peruvian and Chilean ancestry, told us, "If you're not curious, you won't imagine all the possibilities. The more people and cultures you know, the more flexible you can be."

Susan, who described her own background as "boring," says she always wanted to get home from school—where everyone was homogeneous—to be with her friends who were different. "My first friend of different descent," she says, "was a Japanese-American girl whose family was interned in World War II. She and her family taught me to eat sukiyaki with chopsticks. To me, it was tantalizingly exotic."

Court says his mother lived in Russia for four years before becoming an elementary school teacher in San Antonio. She taught Court and his sister to listen and learn. Although they weren't wealthy enough to travel—his father was a bricklayer—she exposed them to new cultures through books. She encouraged them to read about life in the Middle East and other parts of the world.

"Books can take you anywhere in the world," he says. His international career probably has its roots in the attitudes he learned from his mother and the bedtime stories she told him.

We asked Dahlia, a twenty-one-year-old Egyptian who was born in the United States and who lived in Egypt for sixteen years, how she felt when people noticed she was *different* and asked her about it.

"It's okay to ask," she told us. "People sometimes notice something special about me—my accent, the way I look—and that's fine. It's just normal. When they ask, they can learn from the things that are different. If they don't ask about it, I worry that they don't like me."

CURIOUS PEOPLE

Are open-minded

Learn from everything and everyone

Are focused

Are more satisfied

Seem younger than their years

Stay mentally sharp longer

WHAT YOU ASSUME IS WHAT YOU GET

Most of us are aware that our expectations affect our own behavior. If you envision yourself losing this afternoon's tennis match, you are more likely to lose. If you assume you will win, your chances of winning increase significantly. We call these self-fulfilling prophesies. What many people don't know is that one person's beliefs can contribute to another's outcomes.

Time and again, research has demonstrated that our assumptions shape the outcomes. In an experiment, the Harvard professor

HOW OUR EXPECTATIONS PROVE TO BE CORRECT

When Ned meets Zelda, Ned makes assumptions about Zelda. (Perhaps Ned assumes Zelda is clumsy and slow.)
Ned communicates those assumptions in cues to Zelda. (He passes a cup of coffee to her veeeery carefully, and he speaks to her slowly, enunciating each word.)
Zelda responds to those cues by matching them. (Zelda rather nervously takes the coffee from him and spills a bit. She hangs on his words and looks baffled.)
Thus, Ned's assumptions prove to be true. (Zelda is clumsy and slow in their interaction.)

Robert Rosenthal told students he had developed a strain of highly intelligent rats that could zip through a maze in record time. Then he passed out regular old rats to all the students. He told half of them they were getting the smart rats; the other half, he said, were getting dull rats. The "smart" rats became faster and more accurate every day; the "dull" rats wouldn't even leave the starting gate 29 percent of the time.

The biologist Rupert Sheldrake recounts an experiment in which fourteen graduate students administered the Rorschach ink-blot procedure. Half of them were told that experienced psychologists obtained more human than animal images from the people they were testing. The other half were given the same ink blots but told that experienced psychologists got more animal images. People who were tested by the first group saw more humans; people in the second group saw more animals.[4]

In a well-known experiment in a public elementary school, Rosenthal and Lenore Jacobson gave teachers the names of students who, they said, could be expected to perform extraordinarily well during the school year. In fact, the names had been chosen at random. Sure enough, those students they identified as "academic spurters" showed an average twelve-point increase on their IQ scores at the end of the school year.[5]

If you assume when you meet someone that the two of you probably won't get along very well, you probably won't. Or if you assume someone isn't very bright or sociable or interesting, he or she probably won't be very sociable or have bright and interesting things to say. Or if you use stereotypes to predict someone's behavior, that someone will probably fit the stereotype to a tee. On the other hand, if you assume the person you're just meeting has valuable things to teach, that assumption will likely come true.

Jeffrey decided soon after meeting Garrett that Garrett was a fussbudget—too analytical, too controlling, too boring. He was impatient with Garrett and felt that Garrett needed to get with the program and learn to do things Jeffrey's way. His assumptions shaped the outcome—he lost the connection and the client.

We're quite sure that, had Terry Gross been interviewing Garrett on *Fresh Air*, she would have gone into the interview assuming that Garrett was a worthwhile and interesting person with all sorts of ideas and observations and experiences she could learn from. She says one of the best things that can happen when she's talking with someone is that the conversation can cause the interviewee to think of something he or she had never thought of before. She finds it fascinating when that happens.

In our focus groups, we met Mark, a thirty-seven-year-old gay man from California whose positive assumptions make all the difference. We think it would be easy for him to resent questions about his sexual orientation because so many people are judgmental and intolerant of the way in which he's different. But he goes into every interaction with strangers willing to talk about anything. "My philosophy is that I will be offended by *nothing*," he says. "I keep the door open. You can ask me anything. Ignorance is fine. I'll tell you anything you want to know."

"Positive intent makes a big difference," says Margaret, a woman in her forties who attended one of our focus groups. "Sometimes there's a genuineness and an innocence about people when they ask me about being African American. I don't mind if people admit to being ignorant about it. It helps if they have the attitude 'Help me to understand.'"

Ana, who works for La Agencia de Orcí in Chicago, was once teaching English to a student from China, and she was struggling to understand him because of his accent. "It was a big barrier," she says. "I had to constantly ask him to repeat, to speak louder, to slow down." Then she decided to change her focus; she asked herself what he might be able to teach her.

"I got to wondering," she tells us, "what I could learn from him. Could I learn more about China? I asked him about the growth of the cities and about how I'd heard that people were moving from the countryside into cities. I asked him about the growth in his hometown. It turned out his village had grown by like five million people in the last ten years. We spent the rest of the lesson talking about that—the lifestyle, transportation, things like that. The longer we talked, the better his pronunciation was and the better I could understand him." When Ana changed her focus from worrying about his accent to identifying what she might learn from him—his value—everything shifted.

EACH INDIVIDUAL IS A CULTURE

When we first began to talk to friends and colleagues about this book and told them it would be about how to connect with people from whom we differ, many assumed that there would be chapters for various *categories* of people who are generally regarded as different by the mainstream U.S. culture (although we're not even sure what "mainstream U.S. culture" means anymore). We suppose people thought we would include chapters for African Americans, Native Americans, Latinos, and Asian Americans— and perhaps for the different generations. Then we suppose there

WHEN WE ASSUME SOMEONE HAS LITTLE TO OFFER, WE . . .	WHEN WE ASSUME SOMEONE HAS VALUABLE THINGS TO TEACH US, WE . . .
Avoid spending time	Spend more time
Frown, make less eye contact, close our body language	Smile, nod, sustain eye contact, open our body language
Interrupt	Listen intently
Criticize	Inquire and praise

might have been one for gays and lesbians. Then maybe one for people with disabilities. Then maybe a chapter for those born outside the United States. But would there be only one chapter for that whole group of people—who could be from thousands of different countries of origin? The complexity of writing such a book boggles our minds. Worse yet, we believe it would be useless because categories don't work.

Knowing a little about certain aspects of a person—country of origin, ethnicity, culture, the characteristics of their generation, the preferences of a particular personality style, or the core tenets of a religion—can be useful; but everybody's different. There's no getting around the need for knowing people as individuals.

Take Edna, who participated in our Latino focus group in Detroit. Her last name is Chinese. She was born and raised in Panama. Her father was from China, her mother from India. She is a Buddhist. She has lived in Saudi Arabia and Spain. She's an aerobics instructor at Bally's. Which chapter would you look in to figure out how to relate to Edna?

People ask all the time where she came from. One time recently, when she was out with a friend, she answered like this: "We just came from Seventeen Mile Road."

"But I always treat rude people with dignity," she says. "It takes a lot of energy to be kind. I'm a Buddhist, and we believe everyone has Buddha nature. But sometimes I think to myself, 'Hmmmmm, Buddha missed a few.'"

Jeffrey, in his consulting role, felt that he had already figured out everything that would go into the chapter on how to get along in Garrett's organization. He walked into Garrett's office to plan the three-day meeting in Toronto, thinking he was an expert on the topic. After all, he had worked in most of the divisions and had been a huge success. In fact, Jeffrey was a good match for the generic corporate culture there; his style fit with the entrepreneurial thinking and fun, fast-paced work atmosphere the company was known for. The problem was that he assumed Garrett and his organization were just like the rest. He failed to see them as unique. The strategic planning techniques he had used with the rest of the organization had been so effective—and people had picked them up so naturally—that he assumed Garrett could follow his process. But Jeffrey had failed to realize that Garrett was a culture unto himself and that Garrett's division was unique.

Each individual is a culture. Angela, whom we met at the California State Automobile Association, is a good case in point. Impeccably dressed in a red suit with a matching scarf peeking from the pocket, she projects gentility. Every word is clearly enunciated. She describes herself as "an African American advanced degree professional." She says wherever she goes, people want to know what her background is.

"I'm always the only woman, and the only African American woman. And I don't fit the stereotype a lot of people have."

Angela tells us there were a lot of firsts in her family. Her parents and grandparents all went to college. Her father started a construction company.

"In my high school," she says, "there were 800 graduates. Three were black. Then I went to an all-black college. I was uncomfortable in a new culture there. The first day I was terri-

SOME OF THE ELEMENTS THAT CONTRIBUTE
TO AN INDIVIDUAL'S CULTURE

Country of origin

Race and ethnicity

Religion

Parenting

Generation

Abilities and disabilities

Personal style

Sexual orientation

Political affiliation

Thinking style

Values and beliefs

Style and tastes

fied—so many black people in one location! I cried when I went home because I didn't think I could fit in."

After college, when she applied for a job, she spoke to the interviewer by phone. He was impressed with the things she said and the way she said them, so they scheduled an appointment to meet face-to-face.

On the day of the interview, she arrived early and settled into a comfortable chair in the reception area. At 2:00, the interviewer came out of his office, looked at Angela, and returned to his office without saying anything. A few minutes later, he came out again but went back in immediately.

The third time he came out, he looked at her, confused, and said, "Are *you* Angela?" Apparently, it hadn't occurred to him that the impressive voice on the phone had come from an African American. She didn't fit into the categories he had in his mind, probably subconscious ones. At that point, he must have become aware that Angela was a culture unto herself. The interview went well.

Afterward, she sent him a thank-you note on stationery printed on heavy card stock, something she had been taught to do by her mother and grandmother. He hired her.

He later told her his mother had taught him to send thank-you notes on personal stationery. Despite the differences in their ages and race, he became a mentor to Angela.

Sandy, a forty-nine-year-old second-generation Latin American woman who grew up in San Francisco, didn't really know she was Latina until she went to Catholic school. "My siblings were nine and fifteen years older than me," she says. "They were more like older friends." They were raised speaking Spanish. But by the time Sandy came along, the household spoke only English, and Sandy was raised almost like an only child. The family lived in an Italian community, and Sandy always assumed her family was like all the others.

One day at school another child asked her, "Does your mom make tortillas every day?" A lightbulb went off in her head. She went home and asked about her heritage.

"I know about my heritage now, and I'm proud of it," she says. "But if someone thinks I grew up a certain way because of a category I fit into, they'll be wrong."

"There is no box anymore," says Rose. Her parents were Peruvian and Chilean, but her last name is Scandinavian, and people often seem to be trying to figure out how to categorize her. "I don't fit into a category."

NO STRINGS ATTACHED

When you go out of your way to be friendly to a colleague, you'd think he could warm up to you in exchange. Or, when you show an interest in the hobby of someone you've felt polarized from, you'd think she might show a little interest in you. When you take a team member out to coffee and ask questions about the culture he grew up in, you might think he'd ask about your background. But when we're attempting to connect across difference, it's important that we not expect reciprocity. We need to go into each interaction being our best selves—with no strings attached.

Let's return to the case of Garrett and Jeffrey one last time. Jeffrey walked out of the first meeting in Garrett's office with all sorts of expectations *for Garrett*. He expected Garrett to abandon his slow, steady style and become more spontaneous. But Garrett was the paying customer. Jeffrey was there to serve him! It was presumptuous and unrealistic for Jeffrey to expect Garrett to adjust his style to be more like Jeffrey.

The masters connect masterfully with no strings attached. The Steckels shine a light on others they meet, but they don't especially enjoy the spotlight themselves. Héctor Orcí seeks out people who differ from him, but he doesn't expect to be sought out.

One of Terry Gross's most famous interviews is one that went badly. Her guest was the conservative Fox News Channel host Bill O'Reilly. Google Terry Gross and Bill O'Reilly and you'll get about 100,000 hits. Part of the reason people are so interested in the Gross–O'Reilly interaction is that, on that particular day, Terry was not her usual masterful self. She didn't operate from the principles we've outlined here. She seemed judgmental, not curious. She seemed to assume the worst of her guest. She didn't look for a bridge. Gross began by asking O'Reilly about Al Franken's best-selling book *Lies and the Lying Liars Who Tell Them*, in which Franken satirizes and criticizes conservatives. Terry went on to quote O'Reilly's most acerbic critics and ask him to react to the things they had said about him. About midway through the interview, she tried to read from a *People* magazine review that was critical of O'Reilly's book, *Who's Looking Out for You?* O'Reilly accused her of defamation, said she was doing a "hatchet job" on him, and ended the interview. He walked out of the recording studio at Fox while she was in midsentence.

The next day, on his own program, O'Reilly told his listeners about the face-off in a segment he calls "The Most Ridiculous Item of the Day." He said he ended the interview because it got completely out of hand and that he "enjoyed telling the woman off."[6]

There was clearly bad blood between Gross and O'Reilly, and she probably didn't feel she owed him anything—or vice versa. A year later, though, he invited Terry to be a guest on his program— she actually went to the Fox studios—to discuss their NPR interview and her new book, *All I Did Was Ask*. They found little to agree about. But both of them stayed for the whole thing, and the interview ended amicably.

"A lot of people would not have come in in your position," O'Reilly told her. "You came in, and you're a lot smaller than I am. Thanks for coming in."[7]

CHAPTER 2 AT A GLANCE

Bridging the diversity gap requires that we hold a certain set of beliefs, expectations, and assumptions. We call these the core principles:

- *There's always a bridge.* Those who connect successfully in the face of difference have a fundamental belief in commonality. They assume there's always *something* we have in common.
- *Curiosity is key.* Those who connect well are inquisitive. They're fascinated by people from different backgrounds. Their curiosity makes them resourceful.
- *What you assume is what you get.* Masterful communicators ap-

proach each person they meet, no matter how they differ, expecting the best. They presuppose that this is a good person who has valuable contributions to make and important things to say. These positive expectations contribute to successful outcomes.

- *Each individual is a culture.* Masterful connectors tend not to categorize people. Instead, they think of each person as a culture.
- *No strings attached.* Those who excel at connecting across differences don't expect reciprocity.

PATHWAYS TO CONNECTION

As we've discussed, the core principles are the internal foundation for successful connecting, the beliefs and assumptions that support effective behavior. Great connections start with what we think and feel about people who are different from us. Taking the connection to the next step requires us to get specific about our hopes for the connection and how our reactions may help or hinder. Then we need to take action, translating the principles into behavior to span the divide.

We observed masters in the process of connecting to discover the specific behaviors they use consistently to connect through differences. In our interviews and focus groups, we dug deep into the process to determine what people *do* that works. These behaviors we call the *pathways to connection*. Here they are:

- *Clarify your intention.* Knowing what you want to accomplish in the communication ahead of time focuses your attention and guides your interaction with the other person in a constructive direction.
- *Notice your own reactions.* Sometimes our most limiting beliefs and attitudes live below the surface until they are provoked. When emotional triggers kick in or we find ourselves labeling or stereotyping others, it's time to check what's going on inside us to determine whether our responses help or get in the way.

- *Search for similarities.* Common ground brings us together. Finding shared experiences or preferences helps us connect.
- *Use cues.* Picking up on the subtle and not-so-subtle signals others send is a matter of using our eyes and ears.
- *Experiment and adjust.* Great connections rely on continually trying something new, noticing the response, and adjusting based on feedback. Midcourse correction is the rule, not the exception.

Rather than sequential steps, the pathways are choices you might use at any stage of the conversation. When you follow these guidelines, you can connect with grace and ease. Practicing them just a few times will make them yours for life.

CLARIFY YOUR INTENTION

If you think about it in a particular way, this book is about clarifying your intention to connect and then choosing actions to help you achieve that intention. One of the key themes that emerged in our focus groups was that even a clumsy attempt to communicate will work well as long as the *intention* behind the action is a good one. When someone senses that your intention is to be respectful, or that you wish to pursue a genuine and friendly interest in her country of origin, she will be more open to your approach than if your intention is unclear to her. It helps when she understands *why* you want to know more about her.

When you've just met someone and you ask her questions, the intention behind your questions is often expressed indirectly: in voice tone, in facial expression, and in the sequence and direction of the questions themselves. These nonverbal and contextual aspects of a conversation carry their own meaning, a kind of *metamessage* about the conversation as a whole.

For example, let's suppose you ask her, "How do you pronounce your name?" The question has a totally different meaning depending on what emotions your face and voice express and what you say, ask, or don't say following your question. If your eyebrows draw together and down, the corners of your mouth tighten, and you look into the distance, turning slightly away from her, she may get the metamessage "Your name is too different from what I am used to. It makes me uncomfortable; in fact, dealing with you makes me uncomfortable." If she answers you and you say nothing in response and continue to look away, you confirm her intuition that you're uncomfortable with her.

But if you look at her with interest, raising your brows and tilting your head slightly to the side and relaxing the muscles around your mouth as you ask the same question, she probably gets the metamessage "I want to know everything I can about you. There's probably a lot I can learn from you." Following that question with another, such as "Where did you go to school?" or "How did you learn to speak such fluent English?" will confirm her initial sense that you're interested to know more about her.

Connecting across differences carries more risk of misinterpretation than communicating with those similar to us. One way to minimize the risk is to state clearly to yourself what you hope to accomplish, your *intention*. If you use everything you already know about a person to help you deliver your intended message (and metamessage), you'll increase your chances of success.

In chapter 2 we introduced you to the double-amputee Ron Bachman. One day Ron was leaving the bank and met a man who said, "Oh, my God, what happened to you? If I looked that way, I'd kill myself."

Of course Ron was hurt. He resents it when strangers presume to comment on his physical differences. What a different encounter it would have been if the stranger had just paused a moment to consider his intention. Most people would be dismayed to cause further injury to someone who plainly has plenty of adversity to overcome. If we step into the stranger's shoes, our guess is that in the shock of encountering Ron, he instantly imagined the challenges Ron must face daily and felt overwhelmed. He even may have considered how much courage Ron must have to face those challenges and compared that courage to his own inner resources, realizing that his were inadequate. In an odd way, his remark may have been *intended* as a tribute to Ron. But instead of clarifying his intention, he blurted out what first came to mind. We'll never know his true intention, only the hurtful result of his remark.

Terry Gross knows the importance of clarifying her intention before she talks to her guest. "In my interviews, I try to make connections between somebody's personal life and their work. I want to hear about the things that formed them and created the sensibility that reveals itself in their approach to acting, in their style of writing."[1] She used the preceding strategy when interviewing the film director John Woo, first asking him about growing up in poverty, then leading him to discuss his encounters with Hollywood celebrities. Her intention was to contrast his early life with its limited expectations to the glamorous and exclusive circles he came to inhabit.

She also mentions, with regard to her intent, "I like to go into an interview with an idea of what the storyline is going to be, what shape the interview might have. You don't want to force that shape onto the interview because hopefully you're going to be learning new things about the person. But you'll always have a structure to return to that way."[2] Many of those we found most masterful at connection had a similar strategy: they'd form an idea of how they wanted to approach the meeting or encounter, then be ready to flow with whatever the other person brought into the conversation.

Terry Gross understands that her job is to create a backdrop that enables her guest to be the focus of the interview. She sees her role as highlighting what's interesting about her guest for the audience. Imagine the difference in her communication if her intention were to show off her own brilliance in contrast to her guest's.

Terry's clear intention delivers an unmistakable metamessage to her guests and listeners that she is open and interested in what they have to say. The metamessage carries the undercurrent of a conversation, and it is often there, in what is demonstrated but unspoken, that our genuine intention is communicated. We learned more about that when we met Mark Frazier of Openworld. Mark works on projects in information technology, free zones, privatization, and grassroots self-help. He's lived in or handled projects in fifty-two countries, from Bulgaria to Kyrgyzstan to Sri Lanka to Vanuatu. When connecting with someone in a new country, Mark's intention is to create relationships of mutual benefit. Instead of operating in a win-lose mode, he looks for signs that indicate interest in discovering areas of common value. He notices the way people introduce themselves, the degree to which they start off with an interest in finding common ground.

"If they do that in a playful or surprising way that goes beyond clichés or convention, coming at things from an original angle, or they step a little out on the edge to test what they think," he says, "I'm encouraged, and I look for a similar way to respond."

The playful spirit is an invitation to explore further for projects that might provide mutual benefit. "I size up whether I'm with someone who wants to exchange opinions for the purpose of winning, who's closed to exploration, or someone who shares the view that we can find common ground." Mark seeks common elements in each party's beliefs, assuming that people can enrich their beliefs by learning from others. His sense is that, through new technologies and the cross-cultural relationships they support, people throughout the world are coming to realize not only what's technically possible but also what's spiritually possible.

"We're unloading the baggage that hierarchical, top-down systems carry with them."

After years of working in the third world in environments rife with corruption and exploitation, Mark says he has developed a keen eye for "sharks and predators in the room, people who have a stake in rigging economies and keeping them from growing, or who seek to exclude any but their own group from benefiting." His intention is to take steps toward a world filled with horizontal relationships, in which the disadvantages poor people faced in the past need no longer determine their destiny.

It's not only in individual communication that clarifying our intention makes a big difference. When Honda executives approached La Agencia de Orcí for assistance in reaching the Hispanic market, their request was, "Help us earn the *right* to market to Latinos." They believed that the right to sell to a market hinges on a sincere attempt to understand. Understanding helps build a bridge. Honda's intent was to demonstrate sufficient respect for and insight into the Latino culture that it could speak to Latinos in their own cultural language—not just in Spanish, but in the values and images most meaningful to that group.

Similarly, Charlie, a forty-seven-year-old Los Angeles broadcasting businessman, has been in the awkward position of building relationship with new reports who are older and more experienced in the industry. He intends to align with their interests from the outset, to take a journey together in which they both will benefit. "I think of where I want to go. Then I step into their shoes and see it as they do. And I imagine how to get there together. I frame the journey in a way that's palatable to them. I start conforming to *their* way. I think of this as building relationship equity."

Then there's Jaime Ramirez, account director at La Agencia, who remembers his mentor telling him, "Always keep them nodding. Then you can take them wherever you want to go. That's what trust is." His intention is to start with agreement, then to build trust. He also says that his long-term intention is to create "a satisfied client who trusts what we can do for the brand."

In summary, when the goal is to connect across differences, stating your intention clearly—at least to yourself, and perhaps to the other person—can help a lot.

Ask yourself what you are trying to accomplish in the conversation. Your intention might be to:

- Establish rapport
- Communicate respect for the person and his or her experience
- Increase openness between you
- Transform an adversarial atmosphere into a cooperative one
- Deliver value
- Learn from the differences between you
- Overcome hesitation
- Provide reassurance
- Test the waters by introducing a topic to explore in depth later
- Constructively insert a new fact into a problem-solving session
- Obtain information

NOTICE YOUR OWN REACTIONS

Sometimes the barrier that prevents us from connecting lurks inside us, in our perceptions of a person or of the group that person represents. Beliefs and assumptions reside deep in the unconscious mind. Many of them were formed early in life, through experiences in our families and in our native and regional cultures. Ideally, as we have grown and come to understand ourselves and our values better, we have taken the opportunity to examine our beliefs and assumptions and to consciously decide whether they fit the person we choose to be as an adult. Some beliefs are more useful than others. Beliefs that increase our choices are generally more helpful than those that narrow them.

Baby boomers of many races and creeds grew up in families with parents who held overtly or covertly racist beliefs. As they matured, most boomers began to question those attitudes. Racism didn't fit their sense of identity as a generation. That's why sometimes they're surprised to discover a "legacy" reaction, a response that appears out of the blue, from an old belief they thought they'd discarded long ago.

Rachel, a pediatrician in a clinic run by a large HMO, illustrates such a reaction. She comes from a family that includes several Holocaust survivors. Her patients and their parents love her. She was nominated recently for the chair of a department of pediatrics. As the date for the appointment drew near, a colleague told her there were rumors circulating about her professional conduct. People in the department were saying she was too friendly with patients and inappropriately shared personal details with them.

Rachel decided then and there she was being discriminated against because of her religion. One of her fellow nominees was a prominent Episcopalian doctor. "They'll probably choose him," she told herself, fuming. Her parents had taught her that while gentiles might seem friendly on the surface, she had to be careful not to trust them too much. They would never genuinely accept a Jew into the highest levels of their organizations.

As the days passed, and Rachel had time to think through her situation, she found herself amazed at her reaction. There was no evidence that ethnic bias was at work here, none. Rachel prides herself on her analytical skills; she bases decisions on objective data. Even so, her instant emotional reaction was to think that others were undermining her because she was Jewish.

As she thought through the situation, she became aware that her parents' trauma lived on in her and that her emotional responses had a life of their own. That awareness opened to her the possibility of stepping back, looking at the situation more objectively, and taking action based on what was really going on. She decided to talk to colleagues to gather more information about the rumors and where they came from but to reserve judgment until she had evidence that her ethnicity was indeed an issue.

Rachel never learned the origin of the rumors about her, but she did receive the appointment. The opportunity to examine her own reactions and bring them more in line with her sense of identity was her gift to herself.

At the most unexpected time, we might face a situation that elicits a legacy reaction from us. Carlota is a case in point. Beth and Carlota are business partners, social workers, and ardent child advocates. A few years ago they had a huge caseload of therapy patients, children who were victims of sexual predators. The work is fulfilling, absorbing, and emotionally taxing, the kind of work that's hard to leave at the office. Late on a hot Friday afternoon, they decided to go to a movie for some comic relief and to cool off in the air conditioning. They found seats on the aisle near the rear of the theater. They were talking quietly as people entered the theater and settled in for the film. An older man with unkempt hair sticking out in odd directions walked down the aisle beside them. He wore a Hawaiian shirt with a frayed collar and striped shorts. As he made his way through the theater, he seemed unsteady on his feet. He was touching people sitting on the aisle. Several of them recoiled, looking disgusted.

Carlota said to herself, "That old guy's gross, touching people like that! Why is he doing that? That's way out of line. Should we get an usher to throw him out?" She was surprised when Beth jumped up, pursued the fellow, spoke softly in his ear, took him by the arm, and guided him to an open seat about halfway down the aisle.

As Beth took her seat beside Carlota again, she whispered, "He's blind."

Carlota generally thinks of herself as nonjudgmental. But in that moment she believed what she thought she saw—a man who looked like a drunk living on the street. She made an assumption that his intentions were bad, rather than thinking he might be touching people for a legitimate reason.

"Beth is one of the most observant people I've ever met," Carlota says. "She has a big heart and huge compassion. She's done even more work than I have with sexual perpetrators, but she could see beyond the behavior to the factors driving it."

To Carlota's credit, she used this experience to look inward and examine how her reactions got in the way when someone needed help. Her life mission is helping others who face the challenge of overcoming adversity. But in the moment of encountering an unanticipated difference, her legacy reaction got in the way of interpreting the difference accurately and allowing her to reach out.

Fernando provides another example of looking inward and managing oneself. When he moved to Miami from Mexico City to work for a startup ad agency, he had to manage his reactions to a new culture. "It was my first experience in the United States. The culture I came from is homogeneous. I was open to the idea of new cultures, but I had no experience," he told us.

Fernando was raised Baptist, and his Christian beliefs are a big part of his life. The people he knew in Mexico were all very much like him. The biggest difference among them was that some were Catholic, but they were all Mexican and Christian. The Miami agency included people from a variety of cultural backgrounds— Dominican, Indian, Texan, Colombian, Argentine, Chilean, Panamanian, and Japanese American.

"I was alone in this new country and didn't pick my coworkers as friends. We started the agency and became like a family. It put us together like a reality show. Coming from Mexico, I lost family and roots."

Fernando befriended a Hindu coworker. Unlike Fernando,

who considered himself an old-fashioned geek, his Hindu co-worker knew how to handle interactive web pages, and Fernando admired his work and design. On top of that, his new friend was cool and showed him stores and clubs. They even formed a band, with his new friend on guitar and Fernando on bass.

"Then religion came up. We were both young, stubborn, not open to other thoughts. I told him, 'You and your parents are going to hell.' I felt sad and realized that he wouldn't convert, so I *had* to accept him. He was my only friend. I realized I was as strange to him as he was to me." Fernando decided not to try to convert him but to be his friend.

"The religious difference was an insurmountable barrier at first, but I pushed it aside," Fernando explained. "While there were still places we couldn't go together, you learn to hold the differences in reserve."

The end result: Fernando noticed that his reaction to his Hindu friend was incompatible with their developing friendship, forcing him to choose between his judgment of their differences and his friendship. He chose to change his reaction so that he could keep the friend. Deciding to "hold the differences in reserve" was a new choice for Fernando. In Mexico, there was no need to examine his old beliefs or make such a choice. But moving to a new and more diverse culture forced him to grow.

Noticing our reactions also can mean being aware of how our feelings about our own ethnicity can affect our ability to connect with others. Bill, a fifty-six-year-old California-born Chinese American, had to learn to manage his reactions to prejudice as a young man. He grew up in Stockton, where there were few Chinese in the 1950s. The kids called him "Chink" and teased him by making up Chinese words. That hurt. It made Bill feel different.

"My mom spoke only Chinese," Bill explains. "I was ashamed when people looked at us in public. Then in the 1960s, when the Black Power movement began, it woke up Asians, too. I learned to be proud of our culture and characteristics. I began to speak Chinese openly, for example." Bill noticed that his reaction of shame set him apart and isolated him from others. He said, "Each person has his own culture. Most people don't approach you with the intent to offend. It may be ignorance. I decide ahead of time not to take offense." Bill's choice to change his response to prejudice frees him and opens doors to better relations with others.

Adriana grew up in Detroit. Today she holds a position in community leadership where her success depends on connecting with people from many varied backgrounds. She talked to us about how important it is to pay attention to our mental and emotional responses as we connect.

As a Mexican American, she embraces both worlds. "You have to step out of your comfort zone," she said. "Years ago, I was basing all my decisions on *my* community. I was getting tunnel vision. I learned to take a bigger perspective." Taking a bigger perspective is a passion for her. She has a bond with the Mexican community and is proud of her background. "I like to dispel stereotypes," she told us. "The more you know about your own culture, the less threatened you are by differences. It's good to know about your history and roots: that way, when someone slurs your community, you understand it's because they don't know. You can navigate through it. You make it your mission to educate the world."

There are fewer Latinos in Detroit than in other places like the Southwest, so Adriana and her family were forced out of their comfort zone. She also encountered more intermarriage in Michigan than in the Southwest, which surprised her at first. "I had to learn to appreciate how Slovaks and Appalachian whites enrich what I learned in my family," she said. " It was a valuable experience for me to question what I learned as a child."

Sometimes it's our reactions to *others'* reactions that we have to manage. Making a conscious choice about how to respond to

REACTIONS TO LOOK AT

Fear, anxiety

Defensiveness

Self-righteousness

Anger, impatience

Judgmental reactions

Apathy, boredom

Disgust

Disappointment

Blaming

Envy

Intimidation

Denial

prejudice, for example, gives us more control over the situation. CJ is an outgoing, energetic, thirty-year-old third-generation Chinese American woman who works for CSAA, the AAA affiliate.

"I worked in the main office. I built relationships with people over the phone. Then I'd meet them two years later," she told us. "They'd say, 'Oh, you speak English so well.' I'd think, 'Well, yeah, that *is* my first language.' Because I'm Asian, people also sometimes expect me to be quiet and unassertive. I take it as a challenge to break the stereotype." CJ is secure in her identity, so she's confident that she can change people's perceptions about Asians.

The preceding examples demonstrate that connecting across differences requires self-examination. We can prompt ourselves by asking some probing questions. Are the barriers we encounter buried inside our assumptions and reactions? Do our reactions help or hinder as we reach out to others? When we find unconstructive reactions in ourselves, do we have the courage and integrity to change them? Where we find righteousness or defensiveness, is it possible to observe our situation differently and increase the options for connecting?

There are many reactions that can interfere with connecting. If you find them in yourself, it's probably good to look inside and ask whether the reaction is helping or hindering your desire to relate to someone.

SEARCH FOR SIMILARITIES

Richard and Michele Steckel seek similarities that unite the people of the world into a family. Cameras in hands, they travel far and wide photographing children in situations that everyone recognizes and relates to: first haircut, birthdays, sticking their tongues out. As humans, our DNA commands us to respond warmly to children. It's in our programming, and it's a similarity unifying the most diverse people on the planet. Differences between us melt like the Wicked Witch of the West from *The Wizard of Oz* when they are doused in the water of similarity.

Love for children is a strong bond among all kinds of people. Another bond comes from creating similarities by matching each other. Within minutes of birth, mothers and babies are matching each other's facial expressions and movements. Mirroring each other physically develops rapport. When we adopt similar body positions, make eye contact, use the same gestures, speak at the same tempo and volume, we develop *simpatico,* or rapport.

Conversely, we can feel when we're out of rapport with others. They stop matching and mirroring. If you meet a coworker and she doesn't fall into "sync" with you but instead stiffens her posture, refuses to meet your gaze, and answers your greeting with an abrupt "Hello" you know that something's wrong. She doesn't have to tell you in words; you get the message loud and clear.

Matching and mirroring are unconscious ways that we create similarities to connect. When we discover that we both grew up in Minneapolis, or went to the same high school, or support the same football team, or go to the same hairdresser, or know someone in common, the bond between us begins to grow.

Ray, a thirty-something African American, recalls a time when his boss used a similarity to help him through a professional crisis. "When I started in actuarial science, I made a huge error, more than $1 million. I felt terrible. My boss said, 'I made the same mistake when I started. I know how conscientious you are. The good news is that you won't make that mistake again.' It made my error seem human and helped me to forgive myself."

Sometimes you must look further than the obvious similarity to find a point of connection. In CJ's work group at CSAA, there are three African Americans: one is a Southern-born debutante, one a city kid born in San Francisco, and one a graduate of the University of California system.

"They were raised so differently. You'd have to look in different places with each person to find the similarity to help you connect," she says. Assuming people are similar to one another on the basis of only one element of their background or ethnic group risks violating the Titanium Rule. Each person is a culture. These three coworkers may be female and African American, but those facts don't tell you very much about them as individuals. You have to search for that in other aspects of the person: in her passion for sea kayaking or reading Steinbeck, for example.

Similarities can build a bridge even across painful divisions in a family. Roz is a lesbian from California who is of Italian descent. When she "came out" to her family, some of her siblings, especially her sister, couldn't bring themselves to accept her sexual preference. The sisters remained estranged for some years. But Roz says, "Once my sister came for a visit, she found that we had a lot in common as families. She said, 'Oh, they have the same furniture as we do.'" Even such a simple similarity can start to mend a heartbreaking rift.

Johay, a Filipina who migrated to the United States after falling in love with someone from the Bay Area, thinks that language, country of origin, gender, and ethnicity are becoming less relevant in the face of more important similarities. She's in IT, where things change and evolve rapidly. It's also more casual and accepting than other cultures. "What matters in IT is whether you know COBAL or another computer language, or whether you've heard about a new chip," Johay explains. "Age and gender don't matter because everything in IT is new. It's what you can add to the conversation that matters."

In our interviews and focus groups, participants offered suggestions about looking for similarities when trying to build a bridge. There are many kinds of links between people, including these:

- Sharing a geographical connection, such as having worked in New Mexico or vacationed in Croatia
- Enjoying food; good food connects all kinds of people
- Exploring new kinds of wine, coffee, or exotic tea
- Getting or extending an invitation to visit someone at home
- Attending a celebration, wedding, or birthday party
- Coming together to enjoy music or dancing
- Recalling a learning experience, such as attempting to master Spanish or algebra

Charlie, the forty-seven-year-old broadcasting executive in Los Angeles we met before, has often faced the challenge of being transferred to lead a new team. He knows the importance of getting the relationship with his new reports off to a good start. He begins by deliberately building a platform for working together that is based on establishing rapport, matching and mirroring, then looking for common ground in similarities—"Can you believe what happened in the Lakers game last night?" or "My parents grew up in the Depression, too"— and then he takes the connection one step further. He told us, "The relationship has to be based on commonality, the desire to do good work together." Charlie finds the tie to build bonds in their mutual commitment to excellence.

USE CUES

Yvonne, a vice president in charge of the personal-card division of a major credit card company, had a big problem. The company was losing customers. Its research suggested that part of the loss stemmed from a communication challenge: customers didn't understand the benefits of using their premium card. For example, the card offered free primary collision-damage-waiver insurance, the kind a rental car company usually charges for, when customers used their card to rent a car. But key customers, frequent business travelers, were not reading the inserts that accompanied their bills. Yvonne wanted solutions, and she wanted them yesterday. With revenue marching out the door, she and her team had been tasked to reach for creative solutions.

Team members asked themselves, "So how *do* you communicate with a customer if not through the mail?" They wondered if they could use incoming calls to the call center as a vehicle for informing customers about the benefits of using the company's card and for building loyalty.

They met with Lauren, a consultant who specializes in helping CSRs (customer service representatives) connect instantly over the telephone. Lauren watched and listened carefully as Yvonne laid out the problem. Lauren knew she could help. She began describing the various methods a CSR might use to develop rapid rapport with a customer on the phone, repeating key words and phrases, taking note of what's important to customers and addressing their concerns succinctly and directly, using subtle techniques of harmonizing voice tempo and tone with the customer, empathizing before presenting solutions.

Using these methods to connect with customers, the rep could "earn" enough rapport with the customer to build a transition from responding to customer concerns to opening a new topic of conversation—the benefits of the card. Her recommendation was to conduct a test project to train the representatives in communication skills.

But Yvonne wasn't really listening. In her impatience to get to an answer, her eyes glazed over. She was a *visual* thinker, so the approaches Lauren was describing didn't make any sense to her—she couldn't *see* what Lauren was talking about. Lauren's solutions were appropriate for the *auditory* world of a telephone conversation, one in which CSRs have to connect with customers through their voices. The two of them weren't connecting at all. In her frustration, Yvonne shook her head and said, "Nothing you've said impresses me."

Lauren took a deep breath. Obviously, this approach wasn't working, so she had nothing to lose by changing it. She scanned the walls of Yvonne's office. To her left was a photograph of a technical rock climber suspended below an overhang, dangling from one arm. In front of her, on the wall behind Yvonne, were two detail maps, one of Mount Everest, and one of the Himalayas.

Lauren explained to Yvonne that the project wasn't just about improving communication skills in the company's reps. It was about taking the next step as a customer service organization. "It's the difference between a weekend climber and one who perpetually seeks the highest peak," Lauren suggested. "The weekend climber pushes and grunts his way up the mountain. His face falls when he scales what he thinks is the last pitch of the summit route, ascends to the ridge, and sees peak after peak above the one he's just attained. But for the climber who's in love with the climb, that's the greatest moment of all." Yvonne's eyes lit up. She looked up and to her right and smiled.

"I see what you mean," she said. "Let's do the test project."

Lauren picked up on the cues in the pictures on Yvonne's walls. Using that information to construct a visual metaphor based on climbing, she connected with Yvonne.

People we meet offer signals about themselves and their preferences. Anything you can observe about others can be a cue: the formality or informality of their dress, their posture, the tempo and volume of their speech. You can learn something about their druthers from whether they proactively drive the conversation or listen receptively, nod their head or drill you with rapid-fire questions. We are constantly broadcasting volumes of information about ourselves and our preferences.

Sherlock Holmes possessed formidable observation skills that enabled him to capitalize on seemingly unimportant details for the significant patterns and meaning behind them. In the following example, Dr. Watson describes how Holmes used his considerable ability to detect cues revealing a great deal about a gentleman who called upon him for consultation.

I took a good look at the man and endeavored, after the fashion of my companion, to read the indications which might be presented by his dress or appearance.

I did not gain very much, however, by my inspection. Our visitor bore every mark of being an average commonplace British tradesman, obese, pompous, and slow. He wore rather baggy gray shepherd's check trousers, a not over-clean black frock-coat, unbuttoned in the front, and a drab waistcoat with a heavy brassy Albert chain, and a square pierced bit of metal dangling down as an ornament. A frayed top-hat and a faded brown overcoat with a wrinkled velvet collar lay upon a chair beside him. Altogether, look as I would, there was nothing remarkable about the man save his blazing red head, and the expression of extreme chagrin and discontent upon his features.

Sherlock Holmes's quick eye took in my occupation, and he shook his head with a smile as he noticed my questioning glances. "Beyond the obvious facts that he has at some time done manual labour, that he takes snuff, that he is a Freemason, that he has been in China, and that he has done a considerable amount of writing lately, I can deduce nothing else."

Mr. Jabez Wilson started up in his chair, with his forefinger upon the paper, but his eyes upon my companion.

"How, in the name of good-fortune, did you know all that, Mr. Holmes?" he asked. "How did you know, for example, that I did manual labour? It's as true as gospel, for I began as a ship's carpenter."

"Your hands, my dear sir. Your right hand is quite a size larger than your left. You have worked with it, and the muscles are more developed."

"Well, the snuff, then, and the Freemasonry?"

"I won't insult your intelligence by telling you how I read that, especially as, rather against the strict rules of your order, you use an arc-and-compass breastpin."

"Ah, of course, I forgot that. But the writing?"

"What else can be indicated by that right cuff so very shiny for five inches, and the left one with the smooth patch near the elbow where you rest it upon the desk?"

"Well, but China?"

"The fish that you have tattooed immediately above your right

wrist could only have been done in China. I have made a small study of tattoo marks and have even contributed to the literature of the subject. That trick of staining the fishes' scales of a delicate pink is quite peculiar to China. When, in addition, I see a Chinese coin hanging from your watch-chain, the matter becomes even more simple."

Mr. Jabez Wilson laughed heavily. "Well, I never!" said he. "I thought at first that you had done something clever, but I see that there was nothing in it, after all."

From Sherlock Holmes—The Red-Headed League,
by Sir Arthur Conan Doyle (1891)

Most of us will never achieve the masterful observation abilities of Sherlock Holmes, but we can improve our skills. As Holmes said on more than one occasion, "My dear Dr. Watson, you see but you do not *observe.*"

Deciding to pay close attention to what we see is the beginning of observation. Sometimes cues are readily apparent, like the offers in chapter 2: Norma Orcí telling her coworker that she had just moved from Mexico City or Doris's "I'm from Wyoming!"

Sometimes they are subtle. In the early meetings between Jeffrey, the consultant, and Garrett, his client, Garrett offered abundant cues that Jeffrey could have used to great advantage if he were more observant. Jeffrey could have noticed that Garrett wore a golf shirt with no logo, simple khaki trousers, and rimless glasses. Those cues, in contrast with the information that Garrett's position in the company ensured his tremendous financial security, might indicate the following preferences:

- No frills, please.
- Keep it simple and streamlined.
- Status symbols are not important to me.

As they were introduced, Garrett looked calmly and directly into Jeffrey's eyes. Head held high and still, he quietly said, "Pleasure." To an astute observer, these cues might indicate Garrett's preference for straightforward, unadorned business conversation leading from Point A (current state) directly to Point B (desired state)—no detours.

They took seats around the conference table, and Jeffrey attempted to break the ice. "It was touch and go whether I'd even be able to get back for this meeting," he said. "I was in Napa over the weekend for a wine tasting and car race. We drank cabernet from the cellar of William Randolph Hearst. I drove a Ferrari Testarossa that belongs to Richard Branson." Jeffrey reveals a lot in this story, including the following preferences and characteristics:

- Fun is important to him.
- Contingency planning is not important; he'll cut the schedule close.
- He drinks fine wines.
- Exotic cars give him a thrill.
- He enjoys the status of rubbing elbows with celebrities.

Jeffrey's a fun guy, and each of the preferences he revealed might well have served to build a connection with other executives at Garrett's company. That kind of story had worked well for him in establishing rapport with executives in the past.

What he didn't notice was the furrow forming between Garrett's eyebrows (cue for "What's that got to do with this meeting?"). Garrett cleared his throat (cue for "Let's change the subject."). He asked Jeffrey for a copy of the agenda (cue for "Let's get on with it."). When Garrett made his cues so overt, Jeffrey couldn't help but notice, and the meeting began, off to a rocky start.

Jeffrey could have demonstrated that he'd picked up on Garrett's cues as indications of his preferences by matching Garrett's nonverbal cues: his posture, direct eye contact, tone of voice, simple and spare use of words. Further, Jeffrey could have observed Garrett's response to his Napa story and at the first sign of Garrett's impatience—the furrow in the brow—cut it short and gotten down to business.

Jaime, the La Agencia account executive, talks about connecting by reading cues, which he really has to do when he's with an Anglo audience. He tells us that Latinos tend to speak with their hands, speak to people's faces, be all over the place. People from Northern Europe, he says, are more subdued. "My body language can seem aggressive," he admits. "If I'm around a bunch of white people, and I notice fear and concern in their faces, I tone it down. I shut up a little. I even out my tone of voice and be calm. Then I re-engage."

As Jaime's story indicates, different cultures offer different cues for connecting. One challenge of traveling abroad is picking up on cues in a new culture. Something as common and vital as customary signals between drivers and pedestrians on the roadway can be difficult for an outsider to read accurately.

Steven, an IT professional at Orcí, and his friend found themselves playing the role of clueless, and cueless, Americans in Italy. The Italians they encountered seemed rude, as if they were on the take, which made it hard for Steven and his friend to like Italy. Maybe part of their impression came from the fact that Italians in the southern city they were visiting weren't used to Americans. Most didn't speak English and seemed impatient with Steven's and his friend's limited Italian. One day, the two went to the bus

CUES TO INDICATE POSSIBLE PREFERENCES

Hairstyle

Clothing, jewelry style

Accessories
(attaché, pens, electronics)

Grooming
(impeccable, relaxed, disheveled)

Meeting place
(mine, yours, neutral)

Environment
(décor, ambiance, exclusivity)

Body type
(lean/ample, athletic, or inactive)

Physical movement
(how much, what kind, at what pace)

Energy level
(active, hyperactive, lethargic)

Presence
(centered, distracted, scattered)

Posture
(leaning toward or away from you)

Physical closeness or distance

Physical touch or lack thereof

Eye contact
(direct, indirect, duration, intensity)

station to use a pay phone, since there was no phone in the youth hostel where they were staying.

As masters of technical tasks from their IT expertise, they were humbled when they couldn't figure out how to use the pay phone. Nearby, a young man on a cell phone was talking a mile a minute. "He looked unreliable," Steven explained, "not like someone to ask for help." They listened to him for twenty minutes as he shouted into the phone, sounding as if he were fighting with someone.

Steven went on to explain how the young man suddenly came over and grabbed the coin from him, pulled the sheet of paper out of his hand, picked up the pay-phone receiver, and talked to the operator. "He got the directions we needed to make an international call and wrote them on a piece of paper," Steven said, as if still trying to figure it out. "He did all of this with short, almost angry gestures and then went back to his cell phone conversation. We thought, 'Thank you, Masked Man.' " The young man may have been talking a mile a minute, but he also was reading cues from the behavior of Steven and his friend.

As technology shrinks the world and we do more cross-cultural work electronically, we don't have the advantage of reading cues face-to-face. Mark Frazier thinks the hardest thing for people of different backgrounds to do is to build trust. In order to trade with people we don't know, we are inventing new kinds of cues to build high-trust environments. Methods like the eBay commerce system are changing the way we evaluate trustworthiness. Feedback on the system provides assurance that the person with whom we are doing business is reputable.

Beyond systematic approaches to building trust, technology is enabling people who've never met to develop long-term business relationships. Mark has built close business relationships over five or six years with people he met on the Internet but has never met in person.

In one case, he was working on a project on a shoestring budget, and he needed software. He did a keyword search and found someone in Russia who had developed part of what he was trying to build. "But this guy is in Russia," he said to himself. Mark had been reading about the Russian mafia. "How would I know I could trust him?" He visited the Russian developer's website and found that he was offering several projects he had developed free as shareware.

Those projects seemed to Mark to be cues about the developer's intentions. "That doesn't sound like the mafia to me," he said to himself. "It sounds like someone who genuinely wants to offer things to the world. It showed character, a spirit that I really like." The Russian developer was interested in working with Mark, and they've been happily developing both free and commercial software together ever since.

EXPERIMENT AND ADJUST

No matter how skillfully you may clarify your intentions, notice and manage your own reactions, search for similarities, and use cues to identify preferences, connecting well is always a work in progress. We put out a feeler, notice what happens, then try something again, notice the response, and use the response to guide our next move. It's a little like the finding game we played as children, hiding something and then giving the seeker feedback, "You're getting warmer, warmer, no—cooler, warmer. . . . Now you're *red hot.*" Success at each moment is a matter of making an offer, noticing the response, and building the next offer on the basis of what you learned from the previous one. A good principle to keep in mind is "There is no failure, only feedback." Flexibility and persistence will almost surely get you there. Keep going, keep trying different things, and notice how you're doing.

Sometimes you have to "fake it 'til you make it." That's just what Ana, who was born in Colombia, did with her friend Jan from England, whom Ana has known a long time. "We went to a bar and met some Irish people Jan knows," Ana told us. "I had gotten used to Jan's English accent. But I had a really hard time understanding the Irish accent, and they were making a bunch of jokes about England. I played along and laughed at the jokes as if

I were following what they were saying. Before long, I was getting used to the accent, and pretty soon I understood very well."

Ana had several choices in this situation. She could have taken her difficulties as a personal insult or assumed they intended to leave her out or felt angry and disappointed that she couldn't understand them. But she chose to focus on her goal—to be part of the fun—and persist, experimenting and adjusting until she could connect. She followed the *pathways*, convinced that if she kept at it, she'd find the bridge. Sure enough, after a while, she could tune in to the music of the Irish accent and follow the conversation.

By the time Héctor Orcí met with Bill Eagleston, his disgruntled client, Héctor's predecessor had already damaged the relationship. Héctor had to experiment and adjust from the first moment he met Bill. In fact, he began picking up cues from the written communications even before they met. He noticed Bill's tendency to get right to the point, even though in Latin culture there would usually be a long period of building rapport, getting to know each other, talking about family and friends to "place" each other in the social context. Sensing Bill's druthers, Héctor started the meeting by asking him how he saw the problem and why the agency was on probation. Then he listened so that he could pick up on more cues and preferences. Following Bill's lead, he communicated directly and succinctly, assuring him that he would immediately address the concerns. And he did just that.

Milton Erickson was a brilliant psychiatrist and hypnotherapist who got amazing results with patients in a mysterious way. He told them stories, and they changed. His own story has become part of the mythology surrounding Dr. Erickson's genius. His skills at connecting and helping people were partly rooted in his own tragedy. At age 17, he contracted polio. It was 1918, and there was no cure and almost no effective treatment. Part of a large family living on a farm before radio and television were available, confined to bed for years, young Milton had to keep his mind engaged. From his bed, he watched and listened for patterns, try-ing to guess which family member had come through the doorway by the sound of the door closing and the footsteps that followed. Sometimes he predicted precisely how many verbal exchanges it would take for an argument to break out between his siblings after their mother had reminded them to do their chores.

Once he thought he had detected a pattern, young Milton en-gaged his curiosity: could he find a way to interrupt it? He began to experiment. Calling out for a glass of water, he interrupted his brothers before their argument could escalate. Or, by pitching a coughing fit, he would distract his sister in midaccusation. And he noticed the result: what worked, what didn't work so well. He ad-justed his actions on the basis of results, trying another approach and another, until he reached the goal of short-circuiting exchanges.

Nights were quiet on the isolated farm, and the Ericksons had to create their own entertainment. Sometimes they sang hymns, played board games, or told stories. Young Milton began to experiment with telling stories and including characters whose personalities were similar to those of his parents and siblings. He used the infor-mation he'd gathered from listening to them intently throughout the day. He wondered if his stories could change the patterns of their behavior. Sometimes they did. Later in his career, he used these acute skills of observation, indirect description, and leading people through stories to effect great changes in his patients.

He eventually recovered from polio sufficiently to earn his medical degree. Ever fascinated with human behavior, he became a psychiatrist. In the circles of people who still study his approach for guidelines in working with the unconscious mind, they tell a story about his legendary persistence and flexibility.

Early in his practice, he worked in a psychiatric ward in a hospital in Michigan. A young man who had been a patient there for years suffered from the delusion that he was Jesus Christ. De-spite years of therapy with well-educated and -intentioned doctors and nurses who had tried to talk "Jesus" out of his belief, the delusion persisted. The staff considered the case hopeless.

Dr. Erickson decided to experiment. He used his powerful skills of observation over several days to pick up on "Jesus'" cues. Rather than argue with the young man about his identity, he sat some distance away, watched, and adjusted his breath to match the rhythm of the patient's for several minutes. The next day, he moved a little closer and noticed that when he would speed up or slow down the tempo of his breath a little bit, the patient followed. He experimented with this indirect communication, adding shifts in his posture and noticing that the patient followed him unconsciously.

Some of his attempts to get "in sync" worked, and some—for example, changing the tempo of his voice—didn't work. For three days in succession, Dr. Erickson adjusted, doing more of what seemed to create the connection and dropping those moves that weren't effective. On the fourth day, he sat next to the patient and continued to breathe in the same rhythm. At that point, he turned to the patient, saying, "I understand you have some experience as a carpenter." From this point of verbal connection, building on days of concentrated experimentation with nonverbal connecting and adjusting, Dr. Erickson let "Jesus" know that there was a new ward being built on the hospital grounds. They needed carpenters, and he got "Jesus" assigned there. Once "Jesus" was interacting with others in a more functional way, it led him back into common reality, and he was released within a few months.

PUTTING IT ALL TOGETHER: LINDSEY SPEAKS TO THE NRA

Lindsey, a lifelong pacifist, faced a challenge that required him to use every one of the pathways. For him, it was self-evident that violence and coercion were not solutions. As a founding member of a nationally known movement for finding peaceful solutions to problems, he spent almost all his time among like-minded people. Known for his passionate speeches on college campuses in support of the cause, he came into the office after a long weekend to see his name on a date on the wall calendar for a speech to a local chapter of the National Rifle Association (NRA). He almost tipped over.

These people represented the opposite of everything he believed in. They were gun-toting, vigilante yahoos! Why did they even want a speech from his organization? He paved a blue streak through the office trying to palm the speaking date off on someone else. No one would take it off his hands. Frustrated, he tried to find out who'd put his name on the calendar. No one was 'fessing up.

Lindsey is twenty-six, black, and slight of build. He wears his hair in dreadlocks. His fashion style could be called "nouveau hippie"—he often wears a tie-dye shirt, baggy, colorful cotton knit pants, and Doc Martens shoes. His name could be a girl's name. When he tried to imagine the speech, he saw himself standing in front of thirty Charlton Heston look-alikes wearing camouflage, army boots, holsters, and bulletproof vests. They were making fun of his hair, his clothes, his name, and his opinions. His heart sank.

Finally resigning himself to the fact that there was no way to avoid the speaking engagement, Lindsey realized that none of his prepared speeches for other organizations would work for this audience. They were written for people who agreed with his position. He started with a blank slate. He asked himself, "What do I want to accomplish with them? What is my *intention*? What's even possible here?"

They certainly weren't going to agree with one another after an hour's speech. Maybe the most he could hope for was to start a dialogue with them. Or maybe his intention should be to find one thing to say that would make someone in that room look at the issue of gun control in a new way. Perhaps his goal should be to put a human face on pacifism. That would be a small step that might lead to something larger.

Once he started to think about his intentions, the assignment started to seem more interesting. Finally, Lindsey settled on a *specific intention*: to find one point of agreement, no matter how small, a common concern between the NRA and his organization. That fit.

As he began to search for points of intersection between his views and theirs, he realized that he was going to have to look beyond his initial conception of NRA members as stereotypical vigilante rednecks looking for someone to shoot. He was a little embarrassed to realize that his knee-jerk reaction to the invitation was to think of all NRA members as one group and of that group as the ideological descendants of the Ku Klux Klan. Lindsey held a deep conviction that people can commit violence only against those they depersonalize. And what had he done but depersonalize NRA members? He committed to getting his head around meeting each person as an individual, not as a cartoon or a label.

It got easier once he decided he needed to know more about why the group wanted to hear from a pacifist organization. He called the local NRA chapter office to speak with the event coordinator. Peg answered the phone in a low, husky voice that sounded like she gargled with Drano. She sounded relieved to hear from him: "Honey, I'm so glad to get your call. We thought you might not want to talk to us." She explained that it wasn't a speech they were after at all. They wanted Lindsey to represent his views on a panel exploring a range of possible solutions to inner-city violence. "We want to know how you'd control crime without using firearms," she said. Something about her warm and earthy style made it possible for Lindsey to lower his shield.

He was surprised that they were open to his ideas. His impression of the NRA was that they were bigoted, closed-minded zealots. "Note to self," he thought, "reexamine assumptions for possible oversimplifications." Lindsey was doing a good job of *examining his own reactions* and weeding out self-imposed barriers to connecting.

After his conversation with Peg, Lindsey realized that he'd already accomplished part of his intention, or his conversation with Peg had done it for him: he had found a common goal—to reduce violence in the inner city. From this one *similarity*, he was confident that he could find more points of connection. He engaged his creative powers and brushed up on the solutions he'd outlined in a white paper he'd written about the topic eight months ago.

As he took his seat on stage for the panel discussion, Lindsey was a little on edge, but it helped that he felt clear and firm in his purpose for being there. The audience was more diverse than he'd expected. There were some Hispanics, an Asian. About a quarter of the people in the room were women. He recognized two of his fellow panel members, one from the Silent March and another from the Brady Center. As he listened to the panel members' introductions, he watched the audience for responses. The guy from the Second Amendment Foundation used a lot of self-deprecating humor, and the audience seemed to like it. They didn't respond so well to the woman who seemed to take everything as a personal attack.

So when the time came for him to make his first point, he made use of those *cues*. "For those of you who are only here for fashion advice—I know that's why you *really* asked me to come," he said, "I'll meet you in the parking lot afterwards for a minimal charge." The group laughed with him, and they were off to a good start. He spoke from the heart, telling them about events that shaped his point of view: seeing children shot while playing in their yards, holding the hand of an armed robber as he died after being beaten with a baseball bat by his victim. He gave examples that buttressed his argument and used emotion to underline his points. His focus and sincerity were not lost on the audience.

The panel discussion concluded with a thank-you for each member. The applause for Lindsey was sincere and prolonged. Although Lindsey and the gun-rights group will probably never agree with each other about gun control, he left with a healthy respect for NRA members as individuals and a sense of satisfaction that he'd represented his organization to the best of his ability.

Lindsey *experimented and adjusted* once he'd accepted his assignment. From his extensive public-speaking experience, he knew from the outset that he had to find a way to build a bridge. He started by experimenting and adjusting inside his head as he imagined being in front of an NRA audience. He realized that having an appropriate purpose (or intention) for being there was essential. He threw out different intentions (experimenting with each in his head) until he found one that fit.

He also knew he had to get past his own reaction to his image of the NRA members as unthinking, irresponsible proponents of violence. He was committed to seeing people as individuals worthy of dignity and respect, and his initial reaction to the letters "NRA" was anything but a good example of that. Noticing that reaction, he adjusted by making the commitment to see its members as individuals. When he spoke with Peg, he experimented with making a connection with her, and it worked. Seated on the panel, he used what he had learned from her and his fellow panel members (experiments in observation) to inform his own approach and adjusted accordingly with humor and goodwill.

All in all, Lindsey's experience with the NRA gave him a good opportunity to stretch his ability to connect through differences.

CHAPTER 3 AT A GLANCE

Beyond the beliefs and assumptions required for bridging the diversity gap are a set of skills. We call these the pathways to connection:

- *Clarify your intention.* Knowing what you want to accomplish focuses your attention and guides you in a constructive direction.

- *Notice your own reactions.* Sometimes our most limiting beliefs and attitudes live below the surface until they are provoked. When emotional triggers kick in or we find ourselves labeling or stereotyping others, it's time to check what's going on inside us to determine whether our responses help or get in the way.

- *Search for similarities.* Common ground brings us together. Finding shared experiences or preferences helps us connect.

- *Use cues.* Picking up on the subtle and not-so-subtle signals others send is a matter of using our eyes and ears.

- *Experiment and adjust.* Great connections rely on continually trying something new, noticing the response, and adjusting based on feedback. Midcourse correction is the rule, not the exception.

POINTS OF VIEW

In our focus groups and interviews, we pay close attention to *how* people connect or fail to connect across differences. Those who connect well shift perspective, seeing situations from different vantage points. This skill is particularly helpful when we face obstacles to connecting, when our biases get in the way, when we are having difficulty understanding someone, or when tempers flare. When an obstacle appears, skilled connectors look for a way around it. They change perspective by mentally stepping out of their own experiences to observe the interaction as if they were outside observers. Or they imagine what the situation would look like if they stepped into the shoes of the other person, experiencing the situation from the other's perspective.

This isn't the kind of thing that most of us think about. It's a mental skill, something that happens entirely on the inside. But having the flexibility to look at your situation from a different angle can sometimes give you the ability to develop more and better choices for how to approach it.

Changing perspective can improve the quality of your interactions. When you are adept at changing point of view, you can shift rapidly and often. Each time you move to another perspective, you get valuable information, your judgment improves, and you grow wiser. Changing perspectives is something anyone can learn, and most of us already do it in some situations. As with other skills, we get better at it with practice.

THREE PERSPECTIVES:
A PASSPORT TO FLEXIBILITY

When you step outside a situation to see it through the eyes of an observer, you step into third-person perspective.

When you step into the other person's shoes to see things from his or her point of view, you step into second-person perspective.

When you see things from your own point of view, you are in first-person perspective.

Jaime, our veteran account executive for La Agencia de Orcí, describes himself as "a happy, blessed Puerto Rican loudmouth." He has short gray hair and wears fashionable glasses. Jaime's job is to build bridges between his clients—who often need to be educated about the Latino market and culture—and the customers they are trying to reach.

When Jaime and his team present materials they've developed for a direct-mail advertising campaign, they actually put the new materials inside a mailbox in front of their client in the meeting room.

"Our clients open the mailbox, take the envelopes out, and open each piece of mail the way someone receiving it would," Jaime says.

Using the mailbox builds on the client's suspense. "I want to have them begging me to show it to them. And I want to sit beside them and uncover things together," he says.

When Jaime and his team present their campaign materials this way, they are asking clients to imagine they are in the customer's skin, experiencing the materials exactly the way their customer will experience them. Their goal is to provide the client with an *emotional experience* of what it would be like to be their customer. Jaime is asking them to shift into *second-person perspective*. This is one way he connects his clients with Latino customers, customers they are in the process of understanding better.

Julian is an executive coach in the United Kingdom. Sometimes his clients hire him on their own initiative because they want to become more capable leaders. In other cases, an individual's boss strongly *recommends* Julian's coaching to improve performance.

It's always more challenging for Julian to connect with people who don't come to him voluntarily. The differences in this case are not as obvious as skin color or a disability. It's a difference in the power of each person's position. Julian is the coach, the one with the answers. The clients are the coachees, who sometimes come into the first meeting feeling that they "messed up" and need help.

Julian is empathetic. He understands that some of his clients feel that his very presence is a declaration of their weakness. He always begins by seeing the situation through their eyes (*second-person perspective*). They often relax right away when they feel his empathy.

He's making a connection by stepping into their shoes to feel the emotions they feel, deepening his understanding of how they see the job, and experiencing the challenges they face. He listens carefully to their impressions of what's going on inside them and around them, to their beliefs about themselves, their bosses, their coworkers, their customers, their industry, and their company. As he hears each piece of information, he adds it to the mosaic he's creating of The World According to My Client. He tries it on until he can see things the way his clients see them so that he would behave just as his clients do. Once he's done that, he has enough information to begin the work of leading them out of their self-defeating or limiting behaviors and into new ones. And with that much empathy coming from him, they begin to trust him. He's earned their trust through his earnest quest to understand who they are and why they see things as they do. This is a turning point; now the client has become receptive to his suggestions and coaching.

"Next I imagine myself standing about twelve feet away from the two of us, myself and the client," he tells us. "I mentally adopt the posture of an impartial onlooker, arms crossed, my head tilted back and slightly to the left."

From this detached viewpoint (*third-person perspective*), Julian observes the two of them: himself and his client. He listens to the tone of his voice in relation to his client's tone of voice, just as an outsider would hear them. He assesses everything about the relationship: language patterns, body language, eye contact, head nodding, how each person seems to be feeling, who's doing more talking, whether they seem to be making progress or going round in circles in the conversation.

"I get completely new information about how we are doing," he says. "Sometimes I notice I'm pushing her too much, too fast, or getting into her space. Or I hear a touch of anxiety in my own voice. The Observer Julian says to Coach Julian, 'With that tone of voice, she's probably picking up on your anxiety.' So I can coach *myself* to relax, slow down and soften my tone."

Only by stepping into third-person perspective is Julian able to see how he's doing and what impact he's having on his client. It's like having video feedback in real time, only it all happens inside his head. That helps him make wiser decisions about what to do next to connect more effectively.

Jaime and Julian are experienced professionals who connect masterfully with just about anyone, no matter how different. One component of their mastery is their skill at changing point of view. Jaime knows his presentation will be more powerful when he asks his client to see the materials through the customer's eyes. Julian uses his ability to step into his clients' experiences to gain entry into their worlds, even when they are initially reluctant to invite him. And he develops into a better coach when he mentally takes the perspective of a fly on the wall to observe his own behavior in relation to his client.

When you are interacting with someone who is different and you see the situation only from your own point of view, you can miss valuable information. Shifting point of view gives you much more, and much richer, data to work with. Similarities and cues you uncover from second- and third-person perspective form the building materials for your bridge.

Terry Gross uses second-person perspective in her interviews to quickly connect and move into deeper territory so that it's more interesting for her radio audience (that's second-person perspective with the audience). Because she identifies with her guests and sincerely wants to make them comfortable, they open up.

Richard and Michele Steckel use "universal needs and desires"—that's third-person perspective—to connect all people. Their life's work is to present compelling images that change perceptions. In a sense, their mission stands above individual identities and relationships. They see themselves as part of the human family, a third-person perspective.

When he is working with clients, Héctor Orcí shifts perspective regularly. He and his agency have a goal: to be successful (first-person perspective) by satisfying their clients (second-person perspective) better than anyone else can (to evaluate this, Héctor must stand in third-person perspective to survey the whole situation— his client, his client's customers, himself, the advertising industry, and competitors eager to get his clients).

He's been in this business long enough to know that there are ups and downs in the client–agency relationship. "We're people," he says. "We make mistakes. We have disasters, successes, and failures." Each mistake or failure creates differences.

Héctor tells us how he handles things when the client is frustrated and angry. "Every once in a while, we have to drain the poison," he says, "to get everything negative out on the table.

When we sit down for one of these meetings, we offer no defense. We just listen, listen, listen."

"Then," he tells us, "we ask, 'How are we doing in this area?' 'How about that area?' 'Last time we spoke, you were unhappy in this area. How's that going?'"

"Tell me more," he tells them. "Don't hold back. I'd rather be offended than fired."

Then Héctor probes into any area where he suspects there may be a problem. When Héctor is listening and inquiring, he's building the accuracy of his second-person perspective by doggedly seeking to understand the problems. As a result, he can make better and more educated guesses about his client's preferences and how the client will respond in the future. When he says, "I'd rather be offended than fired," he shifts back into first-person perspective—keeping the client is *what's in it for Héctor*.

ME: FIRST-PERSON PERSPECTIVE

First-person perspective is seeing things as you normally do, from your own point of view. It's sitting dead center inside who you are, seeing what you see, hearing what you hear, feeling what you feel, and knowing what you know. A strong first-person perspective is what defines you and makes you who you are.

Leaders take first-person perspective when they set a course of action. They first survey the landscape and listen to others for their insights. After taking second-person perspective in order to understand more deeply, they then step back and look from third-person perspective to get enough distance to evaluate the options and see how their own biases might be playing out. Finally, they step back in to first-person perspective, make a decision, and put a stake in the ground about how to get from there to the goal. It's from their own personal deepest sense of what's right and fitting to the circumstances, which they can only know from being in contact with themselves.

As the Oracle to Apollo at Delphi advises, "Know thyself." The better you understand yourself—who you are, how you got to be the way you are, what's important to you, what you like and don't like, what your triggers are—the better you become at understanding and connecting with others. When you know yourself, you can teach others about your style and preferences. You can keep them up-to-date with your responses. Sharing such information builds trust. This is the reason successful negotiators reveal *more* rather than *less* about themselves and their interests as they negotiate.

Sometimes a blind spot weakens a person's first-person perspective and gets in the way of connecting. One such situation involves Darnell, an associate partner and the only African American in an accounting firm. Darnell isn't aware that he communicates differently with people on the basis of their level of authority. It's a difference he has difficulty overcoming. Two years ago, after he had worked hard for a decade to prove his value, the firm rewarded him with the associate partnership position and a small percentage of shares.

Darnell prides himself on being an empathetic manager. Staff members have always come to him with their concerns, and years ago he took on the role of communicating their needs and wants, especially their dissatisfaction, to the partners. He feels his role as ombudsman has made him a more competent manager, because he truly understands the people who report to him.

He hasn't been shy about letting senior partners know that he sees them as less competent. They acknowledge Darnell's talent with employees; it's one of the reasons they promoted him. They've even asked him to take on a larger role in hiring and managing staff.

Darnell has been especially critical of one senior partner. An ambitious, driven accountant, Cali has given her heart and soul to the firm, working evenings and Saturdays, missing her son's performances at school, even spending part of each month traveling back and forth to China to work on the firm's most time-consuming and profitable project. Her determination to overcome obstacles and the way she focuses on objectives have taken her far in a world that often required more of women than men.

Darnell has told Cali she is unpopular with staff members. He says they think she is demanding. They complain to Darnell that she requires them to spend extra time going over details on reports and making last-minute changes.

Darnell is savvy in his relations with subordinates. He treats them considerately and publicly recognizes their contributions and accomplishments. He often steps into second-person perspective to think about the way his communication affects them. But when it comes to his communication with Cali, who is a full partner in the firm, it's a different story.

"I know Darnell has a lot to teach me," Cali says. "But his self-righteousness gets in the way. I'd like to learn from him, but I can't do it when he invalidates everything I do."

Darnell is blind to his unrealistic expectations of the senior partners. He doesn't realize he treats people differently according to their power. Unconsciously, he identifies with those who have less power than he does—and highlights the differences with those who have more power. His attitude about authority figures probably comes from experiences he had when he was younger—and maybe even from stories that were passed down from his grandparents and great-grandparents.

In his relationship with Cali, it's more important to Darnell to be right than it is to be helpful. His righteousness puts barriers between them. Darnell needs to dig deep to understand his own intentions—why he needs to make Cali wrong in order to validate his own style. Once he understands what it does for him, he can find ways to validate his style without belittling hers. What we don't know about ourselves can hurt us—badly. Darnell's blind spot is keeping him from connecting with Cali.

The model for enriching first-person perspective presented in Figure 4-1 can be helpful in analyzing the poor connection Darnell has with Cali. We've adapted it from the Johari Window, which was developed at the University of California in the 1950s by Joe Luft and Harry Ingham. The model shows four aspects of awareness of ourselves and others' awareness of us. There are things about ourselves that we're open about, while there are other aspects of our personalities we keep to ourselves. We also have elements of ourselves we're not even aware of and aspects of ourselves that others perceive but that remain hidden to us.

A solid understanding of yourself makes your first-person perspective stronger. If you don't know your blind spots, you're vulnerable. The Awareness Model is a tool to help you think about how what you know and don't know about yourself affects your communication and relationships with others.

The top left quadrant—*Open*—represents the aspects of your personality that you know about yourself and that others know about you. For example, Darnell is black; he has short black hair and brown eyes. He's about five feet ten inches tall. He often wears open-necked shirts to work. He speaks in a fairly soft voice but projects well. He uses an extensive vocabulary, and his message is sometimes muddled: "That aspect of being removed from the sensibilities of the front-line staff is a concern that I have had on many occasions when sitting through partner meetings." All of those aspects of Darnell are easily observed by the people he works with, and he knows them about himself.

The other segments represent less known aspects of your personality. The lower left quadrant is *Private*—things you know about yourself but conceal from others. It may well be that these

FIGURE 4-1. THE AWARENESS MODEL.

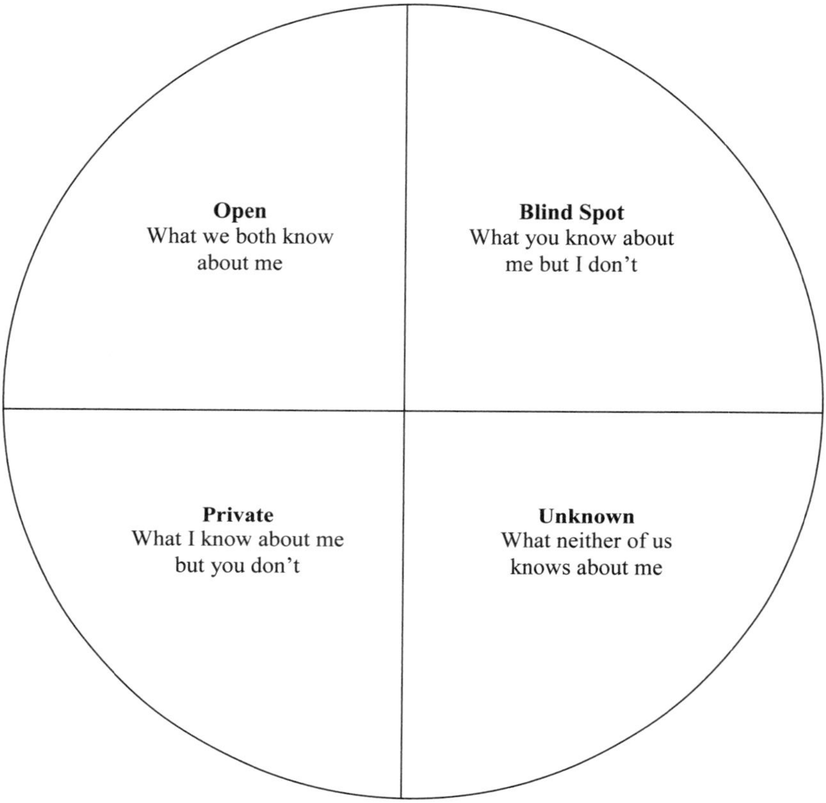

Open What we both know about me	**Blind Spot** What you know about me but I don't
Private What I know about me but you don't	**Unknown** What neither of us knows about me

things are no one else's business! Let's imagine that Darnell has an uncle who was arrested for bank robbery. And maybe he speaks fluent Hungarian, but he doesn't tell anyone because that would feel to him as if he were blowing his own horn. Those parts of himself, then, are in his private aspect.

The two segments on the right side of the model offer a wealth of information for enriching your first-person perspective, knowing yourself better so that you are more effective at connecting through differences. The top segment on the right is the *Blind*

Spot—things others know about you that *you're unaware of*. For Darnell, these are elements of his personality that others know but he doesn't.

Darnell doesn't know that when the senior partners discuss his performance to determine whether to offer him additional shares and how large his year-end bonus should be, their conversation is filled with their respect for him. In fact, they often praise him to his face, but somehow he filters out the compliments.

Darnell is also unaware that he holds limiting beliefs about power and authority. Darnell believes that authority inevitably leads people to abuse those with less power. This belief, lying below his conscious awareness, prompts him to search for evidence to support it. He is constantly on the lookout for authority figures, in this case the senior partners, who impose their needs and desires on those they lead.

Another belief that is part of Darnell's blind spot is that the strong are obliged to stand up for the weak. With those two beliefs driving his behavior, his conscience demands that he challenge the senior partners every time he has an opportunity. Because their compliments and respect are incompatible with his beliefs, Darnell doesn't even hear them.

Until Darnell becomes aware of these beliefs—and the feelings and behaviors resulting from them—he will be ruled by his blind spot. As long as the blind spot is in charge, he will continue to accentuate his differences with Cali and the other senior partners. There will be no connection—and Darnell probably won't get the results he wants at work.

Darnell's blind spot is part of his first-person perspective. Knowing yourself—the forces that drive you, your triggers and hot spots, your values, principles, and beliefs—helps you to be more effective at building bridges with those different from you. When you learn more about your blind spot, you become more fluent in first-person perspective. By examining your beliefs, you expand the *Open* part of your awareness, shrinking the blind spot. In the process, you learn and grow.

The lower segment on the right side of the model is the *Unknown*, things no one knows about you. These can be aspects of your personality that you've never called upon—how you might respond to the loss of a close friend, for example. Or they can be sides of you that you just haven't discovered and that no one else has noticed. The famous painter Grandma Moses would never have known about her talent for painting if she hadn't had to switch from embroidery when arthritis made it difficult for her to sew. She sold her first paintings in her mid-seventies. For much of her life, her painting talent lay dormant in the unknown quadrant.

You can sometimes unearth the unknown parts of yourself by tuning in to nonverbal signals, those feelings or sensations that nag at the edge of your conscious attention—a knot in your stomach, a hunch that pops into your head, a vivid dream.

One woman told us that, after learning about the unknown aspect, she paid special attention when she found herself clenching her teeth in a strategy meeting one day. She figured out she felt uncomfortable whenever her colleague, who had grown up in Serbia, addressed the group. She realized she felt stupid because she couldn't understand his accent. She gets a gold star for discovering an aspect of her unknown. She will now move that element—that she feels stupid when she doesn't understand an accent—into either the private area or the known area. The choice is hers, but finding a way to make her colleague aware of her discomfort will strengthen the bridge between them.

You can increase your understanding of yourself by becoming more aware of the signals and messages you receive from your less-conscious awareness. Attending to these messages brings them into focus and sets up pathways between your unconscious and conscious mind. Just as we alienate others when we refuse to listen or respect what they tell us, we alienate and isolate parts of ourselves when we exile them to the *Unknown*.

Jordan, an HR executive in a firm of about one hundred employees, illustrates the Awareness Model particularly well. Part of her job description—and this is typical of the HR role in some small businesses—requires her to manage the company's facilities. A few months ago, she needed budget information from Elena in finance to renegotiate the lease agreement so that the business could expand into new space in the building.

Early in March, Jordan went down to Elena's office to get the information. Elena seemed friendly enough but stiffened when Jordan told her what she needed. Then she stalled.

"I'm going to need approval from Hal to share that information with you," she said. Jordan and Elena both report to Hal, the president.

As Jordan walked away, she felt a quiver in her stomach. Had she put words to it—at the time, she didn't—the feeling would have told her it was less that Elena needed permission than that she didn't want to give Jordan the information.

A week later, when she hadn't heard from Elena, Jordan left a voice-mail message reminding her about what she needed. In early April, she sent an e-mail. By mid-April, Jordan still didn't have the budget information she needed to negotiate the expanded lease. The firm was in jeopardy of losing the needed space to another tenant in the building, and Jordan was in danger of failing to meet her goals.

When Jordan bumped into Elena on the elevator, she exploded.

"I've asked you for that information for six weeks!" she said. "We're going to lose the space if I don't get it! I don't understand why you have to make this so difficult." It looked like Elena actually smiled the tiniest of smiles.

Elena lifted her chin. "I am responsible for protecting this company from people who might take advantage of inside information," she said, walking off the elevator.

The doors closed behind her, leaving Jordan completely frustrated.

For days, Jordan found herself creating long, angry diatribes in her head, "How dare you?" she would ask the Elena of her imagination. "You are doing this just for the sheer pleasure of seeing me sweat. Well, I'm not giving you the satisfaction."

Jordan reached the conclusion that Elena was using her power to humiliate her. Frustrated, Jordan made an appointment to discuss the situation with Hal. When the time came, she sat down in his office, steaming. She reported on her interactions with Elena. As it turns out, Hal was uncomfortable with conflict—something Jordan knew intuitively but hadn't paid attention to because she was at her wit's end. Hal stood at his window, looking off at something in the distance. He shifted his weight from one foot to another, mumbled something about talking to Elena, then hurried away, claiming to have a meeting to attend.

By then Jordan had stewed over the situation for weeks. Her connection with Elena was in shambles, and she had put Hal in an awkward position, one he hated to be in. When we push signals away or ignore a recurring feeling, we lose valuable time and allow bad situations to worsen. Paying attention to internal clues saves time and extra steps—and makes us more effective at connecting.

If Jordan had attended to her own inner signals—the quiver in her stomach after her first request to Elena, her hunch that Hal hated to be put in the middle of a fight—Jordan could have saved herself weeks of frustration.

Eventually, she did pay attention to her own feelings and the thoughts that were running through her head, so she scheduled a time on Elena's calendar. Before the meeting, she thought through what she wanted to accomplish.

When they sat down together, Jordan told Elena, "I don't know whether this is right or not, but I get the feeling that you're reluctant to give me the information I need. Sometimes it feels like I have to beg and plead and then go over your head to get it. That makes our relationship feel adversarial, which is not what I want."

Jordan was on the right track—finally—and Elena seemed to relax.

Elena explained that her job in finance requires her to protect confidential information. Sometimes, she said, the need for confidentiality conflicts with the need to be open and forthcoming. The guidelines about what to release and what not to release weren't always clear.

"Hal really complicates things," Elena explained. "He tells me one thing one day and then something completely different the next. At one meeting, he urged me to be more open with financial data. Then, the next week, he chewed me out for giving some numbers to one of the vice presidents."

"I'm sorry this has been so difficult for you," Elena told Jordan, "but maybe you can understand my situation." And then—play the Hallelujah Chorus here—Elena actually printed off the financial information Jordan needed. She even took an extra few minutes to walk Jordan through it.

When Jordan listened to clues from the *Unknown* part of herself—her intuitions and the feelings she had first suppressed—and then said them aloud to Elena, things shifted. The relationship became one in which Elena could confide in Jordan about the ambiguous nature of her job and they could work as equal contributors.

By acting on her feelings, Jordan placed herself solidly in first-person perspective—seeing the situation from her own point of view, feeling her own frustration, listening to the conclusions she was coming to in her own mind about Elena. Understanding herself helped her to communicate constructively and work through her differences with Elena.

Authenticity comes from spending time in first-person perspective. When we're there, we base our behavior on our deepest values, and we have access to sensations and cues that serve as guides through complexity. Opening up and showing those aspects of ourselves to others, even when it makes us feel vulnerable to do it, goes a long way to helping us connect with colleagues.

Tips and Traps: Strengthen Your First-Person Perspective

The first step in connecting more effectively with other people is to be completely at home in your own body, that is, fully aware of your own feelings, desires, beliefs, prejudices, assumptions, and tendencies.

HOW TO DO IT

In first-person perspective, you are totally situated in your own skin, seeing the situation through your eyes, hearing it with your ears, feeling your feelings. This requires setting the other person's feelings and experience aside for the moment, quieting down sufficiently to allow yourself to feel, want, need, and believe.

As normal as this sounds, it's difficult for some people. People who are caretakers—parents, nurses, teachers, social workers—in particular find it difficult sometimes to honor their feelings and perspective as fully as they do others'. To stay in first-person, you need to notice and follow up on nagging, persistent signals that pull at your conscious mind. You need to allow all your biases, including illogical, politically incorrect perceptions, to emerge. Paradoxically, you can find your way back to objectivity sooner when you are aware of the full spectrum of your own experience. You must know and honor yourself in order to recognize differences so you can connect with people who aren't just like you.

WHEN TO DO IT

First-person perspective is our perceptual home base. It's always a good place to start and a good place to end up. Other perspectives enlighten and enrich us, but our genuine persona lives here. It's particularly important to shift to first-person perspective when we feel irritation, anger, resentment, frustration, or hurt. Emotions are signals that something needs attention.

HOW TO KNOW WHEN YOU'VE GOT IT

You know you have a strong first-person perspective when you can clearly state your goals, needs, and wants in the situation, and every part of you—your gut, head, and heart—supports them. These are signs that you've resolved any internal conflict.

BEWARE

First-person perspective keeps us grounded in our values and integrity. It helps us to advocate for our own needs and wants. It gives us great information about our unconscious assessment of our situation. But getting stuck in our own point of view is probably the single biggest obstacle to connecting across differences. When we stay inside our own limited view of the world, it's easy to label people as "others" who are "different." If we fail to shift into other perspectives, we lose our ability to assess the *ecology* of the larger system—the impact we have on other people and the environment.

YOU: SECOND-PERSON PERSPECTIVE

When we shift into second-person perspective, we see our situation through the eyes of the other person involved. In a focus group in Detroit, Zack told us about going through security in the Sydney airport not long after 9/11. Security officers singled him out, pulled him aside, and searched him. They took every item out of his bag, ripped the lining out, and examined every part of his person.

Zack is Arab American, and he was probably selected for the search on the basis of his Middle Eastern name and appearance. He felt he was the target of racial profiling. He might well have resented being singled out and harassed on the basis of nothing more than his ethnic background. But he didn't resent it—because the security officer who searched him was empathetic. He apologized to Zack throughout the search.

"I'm sorry, sir," he said. "I realize this must seem unfair. If it happened to me, I would object." The security officer had moved into second-person perspective. Instead of viewing the situation from his own vantage point, he slipped into Zack's perspective.

"He recognized what it was like for me," says Zack. "The delay and hassle didn't seem so bad because he treated me as an individual. He obviously felt uncomfortable with the process."

"I hope you don't leave Australia with a bad impression of us," the officer said to Zack after he'd checked through everything.

Yukiya, who came to the United States from Japan, told us about the strange things people sometimes do when they haven't taken a moment to step into second-person perspective.

"Skillful people don't seem to care about the differences. They talk to me without hesitation. They're casual and relaxed," he says. "Others do weird things like bow with their hands in prayer position. I'm not Buddhist. It makes me feel different."

Bowing to Yukiya builds distance. The people who do this are communicating to him—through nonverbal behavior—that it was the difference that got their attention. Yukiya feels accepted when others adopt second-person perspective, stepping into his shoes and noticing that he just wants to be treated like anybody else.

Most people who come to the United States from other countries tell us that being singled out because they were born somewhere else accentuates differences rather than bridging them. For most people, behaving according to the Titanium Rule dictates that they should accentuate similarities over differences. Second-person perspective enables us to mine for those similarities.

Tips and Traps: Strengthen Your Second-Person Perspective

You gain second-person perspective by imagining yourself standing in the shoes of others, getting inside their skin. If a person is shorter than you are, you imagine how she would see the world from that height. If he focuses on details more than the big picture, you hone in on the petals rather than the bouquet.

HOW TO DO IT

When you shift into second-person perspective, you take on another's personal history, beliefs, and values. You imagine what it would be like to see through that person's eyes, hear from her ears, and feel her feelings, what it would be like to have her experiences and reach the same conclusions as a result.

You improve your second-person perspective through keen observation: you imagine taking on someone's posture, using his gestures, thinking and talking at the same pace he does. You use every cue you receive to enhance the quality of your ability to "become" that person. This is a little like Method acting, in which an actor fully immerses himself in a character, experiencing all sensations as the character would, reacting just as that character would react.

It takes work. Leon from La Agencia tells us, "If you want to connect, you must *put out.*"

Making the effort to step into another person's shoes pays off in understanding and compassion. You improve your own flexibility and range of choices when you "try on" beliefs and behaviors that seem foreign.

WHEN TO DO IT

The best time to take on another's perspective is when you want to increase empathy, understand more fully, or predict reactions or behaviors. Longfellow said, "If we could read the secret history of our enemies"—if we could slip into our enemies' skins and observe things from our enemies' perspectives—"we should find in each person's life enough sorrow and suffering to disarm all hostility." Stepping into another's shoes is powerful; it increases rapport and deepens understanding. Bottom line: shift into second-person perspective when you want to connect.

HOW TO KNOW WHEN YOU'VE GOT IT

You know your second-person perspective is accurate when, faced with the same situation, you would make the same choices and take the same actions the other person would. For example, Shelly is opposed to capital punishment. She can argue tirelessly about the injustices of the legal system and the miscarriages of justice juries have made, especially when those convicted were people of color.

Shelly's friend Daksha didn't have a strong opinion about capital punishment until her sister was raped and murdered by a serial rapist who was out on parole.

In first-person perspective, Shelly opposes the death penalty, but when she steps into Daksha's shoes and feels what it's like to lose a loved one, she can identify with the pain and outrage Daksha feels.

When Shelly steps into second-person perspective with Daksha, she feels determined to make sure the monster who committed this crime never has a chance to deprive another family of someone it loves again. Seeing the situation through Daksha's eyes, she can argue just as persuasively in favor of the death penalty as she argues against it when she steps back into her own point of view. When you can accurately predict the other person's reactions and behavior, you have mastered second-person perspective with that person.

While we can never be entirely accurate in our perceptions of others' experiences, we can continually improve our understanding of them by observing carefully and inquiring respectfully. Method actors step into the character and ask, "What's my motivation?" Understanding what drives the character helps them to immerse themselves in their character's perspective.

If Darnell, the new associate partner at the accounting firm, had stepped into Cali's perspective, he would have come to appreciate her dedication, her innovative approach, her sincere admiration for the staff working under her—and he would have felt her exhaustion. Had he added those perceptions to the ones he already had from his own point of view, his assessment of the situation would have changed dramatically. That dramatic change would have been the signal that he had shifted successfully into second-person perspective with Cali.

BEWARE

Second-person perspective can go too far. When we stand in another's shoes for too long, we lose objectivity. We run the risk of so completely accepting others' perspectives that we join them in their limited views. This happened to a friend and colleague of ours who worked for a consulting firm. She was assigned to conduct training sessions as part of a long-term contract with a telecom in the Northeast.

At the time, union issues inside the company were polarizing management and employees. During a recent strike, a union member had been killed when a strikebreaker accidentally backed his car into him. Feelings about that incident ran very hot. In one session, two-thirds of the participants showed up wearing red T-shirts with a photo of the deceased union member on the front.

In the sessions our friend conducted, participants always referred to strikebreakers as "scabs," and the issue came up in every meeting. In order to connect well enough to be effective, our colleague had to develop empathy with those union members, shifting into second-person perspective with them.

After seven months of meetings, when nearly every person in the company had been through the program, management decided to set up a special session for the nonunion people who had been hired during the strike.

Our friend called her boss to let him know he needed to add a date on the consulting calendar.

"There's going to be a special session for the scabs," she told him.

He came unglued. This was not the kind of language he expected to hear from his consultants. As he saw it, she had completely lost her professionalism.

"My boss," she told us, "wanted to pull me out of that client because he felt I'd 'gone over to the other side.' "

In fact, she had stood in union members' shoes so long— second-person perspective—that she had forgotten this was a word she should normally never use because it violated her personal principles—first-person perspective.

If we overuse or misuse second-person perspective, we can justify others' poor behavioral choices and allow them to stay stuck. Using second-person perspective to gain insight and then stepping back into first-person or out into third will give us the information we need to guide us through challenging situations.

The ability to step into another's shoes comes naturally to some people. They have a way of being able to get into someone else's skin to see the world the way that other person would. But everyone can do it with practice. If you're looking for a bridge, you can virtually always find it by changing into second-person perspective.

THEM: THIRD-PERSON PERSPECTIVE

At a hospital in south Florida, Arnie, JT, other doctors, and administrators are serving on a task force to reduce the number of patients who walk out of the emergency room without ever seeing a doctor. The wait for an examining room and doctor often lasts many hours and seems interminable. If patients need imaging or tests, it can take even longer, so patients leave, disgruntled.

JT heads up the emergency room. He's a soft-spoken, easy-going fellow with a southern accent who likes to go with the flow and give things plenty of time to unfold. He asked Arnie, a radiologist, to serve on the task force because Arnie's a smart guy known for whipping his department into shape. Arnie also identifies with the underdog—in this case, the disgusted ER customer.

Arnie's an excitable guy—energetic, enthusiastic, and outgoing. When something needs to be done, he always has a better way. He grew up in New York City. His family struggled financially, but he always knew he wanted to be a doctor. Arnie put himself through medical school working in hospitals, starting as an orderly.

JT and Arnie are about as different as two doctors can be; if they needed to hail a taxi, Arnie would be out in the middle of the street, shouting and gesturing until a cab screeched to a halt. Meanwhile, JT would be sitting on a bench in the shade, waiting until somebody asked him if he needed a ride.

The ER problem weighs heavily on JT. He's under a lot of pressure from the administration to fix it. He's done everything he could think of to improve things—he eliminated one station for processing insurance forms, developed a system for updating people on wait times, and contracted with hospital-based physicians to double up on weekend nights. He paid for customer-service training for the front-desk staff to ensure that they would extend courtesy to patients during check-in.

As the task force meeting progresses, Arnie begins to get excited. He's got lots of ideas and has tossed out three of them to JT in the past ten minutes. As Arnie gets more excited, he leans further forward, speaking with more animation. His voice gets louder and faster. Each time he comes forward, JT pulls back, the tendons in the front of his neck sticking out. Before long, JT's about to tip over backward in his chair. Arnie has good input, but JT is overwhelmed, and Arnie's not noticing that the more enthusiastic and expressive he becomes, the more JT retreats.

What Arnie needs to do is back off and let JT process what he's already said. But he doesn't see that. If Arnie could detach himself from his own point of view and watch the conversation as if he were a fly on the wall—third-person perspective—it would be obvious to him what he should do. Seeing his approach from the point of view of an observer would reveal that he's being pushy. From the observer perspective, he would realize that JT would welcome his ideas if he just relaxed a little and delivered them more slowly.

Third-person perspective would allow Arnie to let go of the emotional intensity that's pushing JT away. When we step back and look at our situation as a third party would, we naturally become less attached to our own point of view. We get some distance. With the detachment that third-person perspective would give him, Arnie could see that his approach is making JT defensive and uneasy. He could coach himself to use other alternatives: to slow down, ask JT a question, give JT a chance to digest the input, offer to write the suggestions on a flip chart, or give another member of the group a chance to offer some thoughts.

From this perspective, Arnie could see that what he's doing isn't working. He could follow the adage *If what you're doing isn't working, try something else.*

Third-person perspective is particularly useful when we are

overcome with emotion, when we are taking something too personally, or when we're stuck and need to find other alternatives.

Tips and Traps: Strengthen Your Third-Person Perspective

Stepping out of the immediate situation and looking at yourself and the person you are trying to connect with as if you were an objective third party can help you adjust your behavior and improve your chances of being successful.

HOW TO DO IT

Step into third-person, or observer, perspective by imagining how you would see yourself from a distance. You can do this in a number of ways. You can imagine what you would see right now if you were standing behind yourself watching as you read this book. You can imagine you're a fly on the wall watching yourself reading. You can imagine a movie with you on a big screen, and you're sitting in the audience watching. You can imagine you're someone else, standing along the sidelines, observing. These are all ways of getting third-person perspective.

Now think of the last difficult conversation you had with someone. How would the two of you have looked to a bystander witnessing the interaction? Notice how the strong feelings you may have had when you were in the conversation diminish when you see things as if you were an observer.

WHEN TO DO IT

The third-person perspective is most useful when there is a danger that your emotions will take over. It gives you a chance to gather your thoughts and insights to balance the feelings.

Another time to shift into third-person perspective is when you need information about how the relationship is going, how the two parties or "characters" in the film are doing. Third-person perspective gives you a rational assessment so you can coach yourself to be more effective.

HOW TO KNOW WHEN YOU'VE GOT IT

You will know your third-person perspective is strong when you can describe the appearance and behavior of each person in the relationship symmetrically and when you are no more aligned or partial to one party than the other. When you can describe yourself and your behaviors with impartiality and detachment, you will have the full benefit of third-person perspective.

BEWARE

Third-person perspective detaches us and gives us space to come up with more effective choices. But if we get stuck in third-person perspective, we can come across like Data in *Star Trek*. Data was an android, and he was great at processing information, but he didn't have a human, emotional side. Third-person perspective, if overused, makes us seem disconnected, robot-like.

Use third-person perspective to give yourself options, to find another explanation, to help identify the part you play in the problem. Then step back into your own skin and get back in the game with new insights and choices. You'll be amazed at your ability to turn things around.

PUTTING IT ALL TOGETHER: A PROFILE OF NIKKI MOSS

Nikki Moss, supervisor of organizational learning for DTE Energy, in Detroit, Michigan, is exceptional when it comes to connecting with people who differ from her. She manages the training curriculum, schedule, and facilities; handles requests for team-building; leads her team of seven—they provide training, workforce development, and career development—and does all the regular administrative stuff that comes with being a supervisor.

When we studied Nikki's formula for connecting across differences, we found that a major ingredient is her strength in the three perspectives. She reaches out every day from her African American cultural perspective to coworkers, clients, and strangers from other cultures. When she learned that a Japanese American woman she met at a community meeting offers tea ceremonies in her home, Nikki was the first to sign up. After encountering Ron Bachman, the double amputee, at a diversity session in the local schools, she convinced her boss to bring him to DTE. She was the one to conceptualize and implement a "deep-dive diversity lecture series" at DTE, where the first speaker was Jane Elliott, originator of the well-known diversity activity Blue Eyes Brown Eyes.

Her pride in who she is—her first-person perspective—provides the foundation she reaches out from. Her two sons and her marriage of thirty years ground her. Although Nikki never imposes her beliefs on others, she is deeply religious. The huge Afrocentric church she belongs to fills her with wonder and rekindles her faith.

As a bridge builder between cultures and human beings, Nikki notices nuances and then lends support with compassion, wisdom, and insight. On a typical day, before she can even get her cup of tea—with lemon and sugar, please—one of her team members asks to see her for five minutes. An hour later, they've completed several tasks they didn't plan to do. Colleagues take their problems to Nikki because she's masterful at shifting into second-person perspective and looking at issues empathetically.

Nikki's job isn't always easy. For more than a decade, she has taught diversity courses at DTE that don't sidestep issues. The discussions can turn emotional, which is exactly when Nikki shifts into third-person perspective. By stepping out of the discussion to observe the words, thoughts, emotions, interactions, and body language of the participants and herself, she finds better options for facilitating the workshop successfully.

CHAPTER 4 AT A GLANCE

Changing your point of view or perspective can help you to connect with others. Try these tips:

- Choose from three points of view: first-, second-, and third-person perspective.
  - First person: seeing an interaction from your own viewpoint.
  - Second person: seeing an interaction from another's viewpoint.
  - Third person: seeing an interaction from an observer's viewpoint.
- Being well-connected to ourselves requires that we develop acute awareness of the signals we receive from the less conscious parts of ourselves. The unconscious mind communicates through nonverbal channels—feelings, dreams, symbols, and intuitions at the edges of our awareness.
- The Awareness Model depicts known and unknown aspects of our selves. Be aware of what you and others both know and of your blind spots—what others see but you don't, areas that may remain unknown to you and others, and what you know and others don't.

WORKING WITH
DIFFERENCES IN GROUPS

In our work in the United States and around the world, we've found ways to connect in the face of differences large and small. It isn't always easy. Sometimes we have to push ourselves through the tendency to cling to comfort and familiarity. Connecting in a new country or context when we are the ones who're different can be profoundly *un*comfortable at first. We feel awkward. People don't behave as we expect. They move their arms and hands and legs in unfamiliar gestures. Their eyes don't meet ours. Or they don't seem to move at all. They don't speak when we expect them to speak, or they speak when we are supposed to be the ones doing the talking. Then they speak, and we are not sure what they mean. We want to relate to them, but we don't know exactly what to say or do. It's hard to tell if we're connecting. It's all so disconcerting. We feel off balance, like the *other*. And so we are.

The great psychologist Virginia Satir often spoke about familiarity as one of the most compelling forces in human nature. She observed that most people seek the known and shun and fear the unknown. But Satir found that the differences between us are not so terrible.

What made it possible for her to go into the unknown, she said, ". . . is that I've got eyes, ears, skin. I can talk, I can move, I can feel, and I can think. When I give myself permission to say all my real yesses and no's, I can move anywhere . . ."[1] She advised that never having to pretend to know what one doesn't know, never having to say yes when feeling no, and never having to say no when feeling yes is what makes us most effective in coping.

OPENING YOUR PRESENTATION

For those of us who lead groups of people across any kind of boundary of difference, the task of connecting is even greater. Groups are composed of individuals, and the challenge in connecting is always an individual one: to gain rapport and to create a safe and free environment for participation. Your mission as a group leader is to create rapport with the majority of individuals in the group. It's not possible to sit down with each person, find out about her or his preferences, and tailor your presentation for individuals. So, how do you proceed?

You build bridges with bricks of similarity that may apply to many individuals in the group and call them to attention. Finding similarities early in your presentation sets a tone of connection from the start. Have the members of the group just been through a merger? Do they share a profession and therefore face certain similar challenges? Thank goodness there are myriad similarities available to build upon.

As audience members anticipate your presentation, they carry certain hopes into the room, whether they could articulate them or not.

"I hope the presenter will respect me and my culture. I hope she will find us interesting. I hope she will be open to learning from me and from my group and realize how much she can benefit from getting to know us. I hope she won't hold herself and her group as superior to us. I hope she will like our country/town/city/village/school/organization and be able to see what is admirable in how we live and what we are doing. I hope she will see who we are: what we value, the contribution we make. I hope she will be sympathetic to our efforts to make a positive difference, sometimes under trying circumstances and stultifying limitations. I hope she will have done her homework so that she knows something about us before she presumes to teach us about her topic. I hope she won't be afraid of the differences between us and therefore become dictatorial, defensive, pushy, preachy, or dismissive. I hope she will be flexible enough to pick up on the signals when she is connecting with us and when she isn't, and adjust her behavior accordingly. I hope she will be credible and competent, but approachable and human as well."

KEYS TO CONNECTING IN GROUPS

- *Do your homework. Learn enough about your audience to demonstrate your interest and respect.*
- *Establish rapport and credibility in your opening by touching on their hopes right from the start.*
- *Keep your eyes and ears wide open to the feedback you are getting. Learn to read their cues. Sincerely ask for their help. Adjust throughout your presentation based on feedback.*

Your daunting task is to fulfill as many of those hopes as possible. Fortunately, it's not as hard as it may seem. The critical window for connecting is the first three minutes. Your opening should include the following components, not necessarily in this order:

- *A warm greeting.* The most powerful element of your communication is not what you say in words. It's the *state of being* you project as you greet the group: clear, confident, warm, open, alert, anticipating a positive experience and result. Give yourself time and permission to connect strongly with several individuals in different locations in the room—in the front, in the back row, on the left and right sides of the group at a minimum. Make eye contact and linger for just a moment. Your intention at this stage is to offer each person a moment of full *recognition.* Nonverbally, you are saying, "I see you. I'm glad to meet you." Your connection with at least a few members of a large group will deliver the message that you are open and interested in connecting.

- *An expression of appreciation* for the opportunity to meet with group members and experience their culture. This may include mentioning some aspect of their country/culture that is new and delightful to you.

Your sincere interest and appreciation, communicated in the emotional tone of your opening statement, will convey your hopes and intentions for the presentation and the value participants will gain from attending.

Let the group know that you hope to connect, to learn from it and from its culture. Sometimes it helps to say something like, "I'm excited about the opportunity to be here, to learn about you and your culture. I may need your help, though. I'm in the early stages of learning about you. While my intention is always to be respectful and appropriate, I may make mistakes or do things that don't work well here. Will you do me the honor of letting me know so that I can connect well with you?"

In some parts of the world, Americans in particular have a reputation for coming across as *too* self-confident, even arrogant.

POSSIBLE TOPICS FOR MAKING A CONNECTION

- *Places of interest*
  - *Shrines*
  - *Monuments*
  - *Natural wonders*
  - *Scenery*
  - *Antiquities*
  - *Business parks or centers of innovation*
  - *Theaters*
  - *Restaurants*
  - *Museums and galleries*
- *The hospitality of your sponsors or hosts*
- *Aspects of the local culture*
  - *Food*
  - *Dress*
  - *Language*
  - *History*
- *Accomplishments: a fast transit system, clean streets, beautiful parks and gardens, incredibly fresh fruits and vegetables, a rich folk culture with songs or dance or tales transmitting timeless values.*

To counter that reputation, we've found that expressing a bit of humility in the face of difference helps. Soliciting cultural input early in the presentation goes a long way to buying forgiveness if and when you violate a cultural boundary.

Humor also can be an effective way of opening this topic. If it fits your style, you might consider saying something like, "Please realize that I operate under a slight handicap: I'm American. We are isolated geographically. Our country is huge and in some ways overbearing. Please take me on as a special project. I'm willing to learn, just slightly culturally disadvantaged in doing so. I will greatly appreciate your cooperation and assure you I'll welcome your feedback. It's your opportunity to adopt an Ignorant American today." Caveat: this kind of self-effacing humor works well once you've already established some credibility. Without credibility, it may not come off well.

READING CUES IN GROUPS

Of course, as you are speaking to the group, you want to watch carefully for cues indicating how your opening is being received. Note whether people are making eye contact with you or looking away (a sign that you may not be connecting, depending on the culture). Observe facial expressions to see if they're receptive, skeptical, detached, or engaged. And watch body language. Are they sitting still—which usually means they're attentive—or shifting around in their seats? The cues serve as your guidance system. When the feedback suggests you are connecting, do more of whatever you are doing at that moment. When you begin to lose the group, try a different approach.

It's also important to learn to read new cultural cues accurately. People in some cultures are much less demonstrative than those in others, and cues can differ on the basis of culture, even cultures that have much in common. When we first started working in Scandinavia, we'd scan the group for cues, and, to our dismay, we saw little in the way of recognizable responses. People seemed to sit like logs, stone-faced, watching us like bugs pinned to a board. We amped up the volume, making our delivery more dynamic. No observable response.

Approaching the sponsor at the first break, we asked, "What's wrong? We're dying up there. They hate us! How are we offending them?"

The sponsor laughed. "I'm hearing from them that they like you very much. But they're *Norwegians*. They don't express themselves in a very overt way." She told us a joke to illustrate her point: "How can you tell if the Norwegian you're talking with is an extrovert or an introvert? He's an extrovert if he looks at *your* shoes." Once we understood that we had been misreading their cues, we could tune in to and perceive the much more subtle signals to read the audience more accurately.

After working in Norway for a while, we began to discover that the groups and individuals we met were shaping our behavior in many ways. Our gestures became smaller. Our faces were less broadly expressive. We toned down the volume and tonal range of our voices. At one point, we even found ourselves using a unique Norwegian nonverbal expression. Norwegians, especially Norwegian women, sometimes use a quick, sharp, and sudden intake of breath, a reverse whisper that means, in a most delightful way, "I understand what you are saying." It's almost a physical expression that they have literally taken your point in. We've never observed that cue in another culture.

Working in Latin America or southern Europe, we have no problem reading cues. These cultures are vibrantly expressive, and group members there broadcast their feedback in mobile bodies, demonstrative faces, and broad gestures.

Many years ago, working in England for the first time, we also were concerned when we noticed that several group members didn't make eye contact with us. They looked down almost the entire time. We couldn't quite tell what was going on. Were they asleep? Were they offended by something that we said? After a while, we noticed that the cues didn't seem to indicate, as they would in the United States, that these people were tuning us out.

We perceived some clear signs that they were indeed following us. They laughed at one of our jokes and would nod occasionally. Then we got it: they were *listening intently* rather than watching. In England, a larger proportion of the population than that in the United States processes information primarily through the *auditory* system rather than through the visual. British culture at that time, and less so now, was much more adept at using the auditory system than American culture. We suspect that one reason for this disparity between our cultures is that being able to *hear* differences in accent and grammar was one way to determine social class—a crucial skill for social survival—in Britain. Because our educational system has had a more leveling effect, Americans tend to read social class through visual cues: clothing, haircut, and possessions.

This book isn't about how to deal with specific cultural differences. We mention examples to illustrate the point that being new to a culture means learning to pick up on, accurately interpret, and respond to cues that may differ dramatically from those in your home culture. We do suggest that you learn something about the culture before you lead groups in a new country: a few words of the language and common gestures, something about what people are proud of in their culture, and how their expectations might differ from those of your own culture, at a minimum. Knowing that you will have new cues to read in a new culture will help you connect more successfully there.

HELPING DIVERSE GROUPS CONNECT

The preceding guidelines and examples can help when you are different from the homogeneous group you are leading. But what about when the members of your group differ from one another?

In this situation, you face the same challenges as when you are the one who is different—for example, connecting well from the start, developing rapport, demonstrating credibility, creating safety for the group in the learning environment, reading and responding to cues, and experimenting and adjusting your behavior on the basis of feedback.

In addition, you face the task of helping members connect well with one another and building a cohesive culture through their differences. Your challenge will change according to the differences among group members. If we take seriously our adage that each individual is a culture, then all groups are composed of people who differ from one another.

When someone comes into a group for the first time, he usually carries some of the following questions into the room with him, often well below the level of conscious thought:

- Will this be a valuable experience? Will I gain something from participating?
- Will I be safe here? Will it feel safe to learn? Will the atmosphere be competitive? Will I be put in a situation in which I could be embarrassed or exposed? Will the presenter create a sense of community in the group? Or will there be cliques and hierarchy in the group?
- Who else will be here? What will they think of me? What will I think of them? Will I fit in and connect with other group members? Or will I feel isolated?
- Will it be interesting or boring?

To build a successful and cohesive group culture, you as presenter must answer those questions in some way soon after the group forms. Fortunately, there are many ways to help the group members unite and bond. The goal is to bring the group members' differences to their attention and celebrate them. The message you are attempting to deliver is "Isn't it great to have this variety and richness among us?"

Something as simple as having participants introduce themselves by describing an unusual experience or characteristic can serve several purposes:

- Ensuring that each person's voice has been heard in the group
- Highlighting and welcoming differences
- Creating a level playing field, a nonhierarchical community

Another way to help the group bond is to use social mapping. For example, have the group form a visual representation of the globe by imagining a map of the world on the floor, and ask the members to stand on their "city" or "country" of origin as they introduce themselves. Or ask group members to place themselves on a spectrum from low to high familiarity with the subject matter of the class. Then briefly poll group members from various points along the spectrum about what made them choose to place themselves in a particular spot. Take care to assure those who are less familiar with the content that they have important contributions to add to the group's learning. These kinds of activities establish an expectation that differences will make the learning environment rich and lively.

BRIDGING DISAGREEMENT IN A GROUP

When you lead a group that has a history of conflict or controversy, or when you anticipate that conflict is likely to emerge in the group, two of our principles can help build a bridge between factions. Clarifying intention and searching for similarities from the outset will help the group bond around common purpose. We've found that the strength of that initial bond can make it safe for group members to explore highly controversial issues and air strong differences in an atmosphere of respect and appreciation.

Building that bond begins with drawing the group's attention to common ground, especially common intentions, very early in the meeting. You might choose to acknowledge the differences, then lead the group members to focus on what they share. For example, you might say something like, "I know you've had a hard time coming to agreement about how to launch the campaign, the specific action plans that will lead us to the result *we all want*. Feelings ran pretty high about those differences in your last meeting. It's important to start by taking a moment to remember that we are committed to achieving the same objectives and that the passion with which we differ with each other is only a reflection of how deeply we share the dedication to this common purpose. How can we work together from the outset to keep that in mind as we explore how to accomplish our goals?" From here, you might develop a list of working agreements, ground rules for the discussion, that will support the group in airing differences while maintaining respect and goodwill.

In *How Great Decisions Get Made,* Don Maruska recommends opening such a group with an invitation to explore hopes. He writes, "Many groups are hope-less. They don't lack potential, but they do lack clarity about what's truly important to them. This deficiency blocks group members from engaging with one another, discovering effective solutions, and working together effectively. You can turn around any troubling group situation by asking participants two questions: What are your hopes for the meeting? Why are they important to you?"[2]

In taking this approach, Maruska deftly turns the group's attention away from specific positions on issues to the intention, or purpose, behind the meeting or project. Once the group members find common ground at the more general level, on the hopes they share, it's easier to come to agreement on the specifics.

Maruska's strategy capitalizes on the power of seeking alignment rather than agreement. Yasuhiko Genku Kimura, former Zen Buddhist priest and founder of Vision in Action, sees the future of the world as depending on our ability to work with one another to pursue common hopes through differences in beliefs and point of view. "Alignment is congruence of intention; whereas agreement is congruence of belief. People who differ in their beliefs can align in their intention, turning their diverse points of view into a common asset. No more do we need or can we afford the usual politics of opinion-domination, of agreement versus disagreement, which is subverting the integrity of human unity and endangering the future."[3]

Gaining alignment in a group requires the facilitator to take a third-person perspective, staying above the squabble of differing opinions, to see what the parties share in common intention, weaving differences into a tapestry of common design at the level of intention.

Occasionally, the situation seems to call for even stronger measures. We've been asked to lead groups in which key stakeholders were so polarized that even the idea of holding a meeting was objectionable to them. In that case, we've found it necessary to find a way to connect and to span differences ahead of the meeting itself. One strategy that's worked well is to set up a conversation with the "negative thought leaders," those in opposition. We ask them to share their perspective. We listen hard. Every time, we find that what they have to say adds vital information to what we already know. We often ask them to help us design the meeting or give us ideas we can incorporate into our approach. We use most of our principles and pathways in this conversation:

- There's always a bridge. *I can find ways to connect with this person.*

- Curiosity is key. *I wonder what her perspectives are on the issue. What experiences might she have had that would lead her to feel so strongly that she doesn't even want to be in the same room with people who feel differently?*

- What you assume is what you get. *She has good reasons for how she feels. She's well-intended.*

- Each individual is a culture. *She may have a unique take on this issue or there may be personal reasons unrelated to the topic that are motivating her.*

- No strings attached. *I'll extend the offer of listening, honoring her perspective and taking responsibility for bringing that perspective into the room. But I don't assume she'll do the same for me or for others in the group.*

- Clarify your intention. *I want to find out what she needs in order to participate. I want to discover enough about her perspective that I could represent it well in the meeting, even if she decides to decline the invitation to attend.*

- Notice your own reactions. *If I continue to think of her as a fly in the ointment, a "negative thought leader," it will stand in the way of building a relationship with her. I have to shift this. Clearly, she's someone who brings vital pieces of the puzzle into the room. I'll redouble my commitment to search for her positive intention and give her the benefit of the doubt.*

- Search for similarities. *What does she have in common with other members? Where's the common ground? How can I lead the conversation from the level of specific—and opposing—positions to the purposes or intentions she shares with other group members?*

Our experience has been that hearing that person out, stepping into her shoes, and incorporating her input makes it possible for the group to have a meaningful conversation about the real issues that leads to breakthrough. This strategy also can work during the meeting, either in an off-line conversation, or in abbreviated form in front of the group.

PUTTING IT ALL TOGETHER: A CONVERSATION WITH JONATHAN FOX

Jonathan Fox is the founder of Playback Theatre, a form of improvisational theater in which audience members are invited to sit in a seat next to the stage and tell a story from their lives. Actors then enact the story on the spot with no rehearsal or discussion. Playback Theatre strikes a universal chord and is practiced around the world. A Playback Theatre performance reminds us that the experiences that most isolate us—embarrassment, personal loss or gain, the discovery of a new idea—are shared in spirit.

We asked Jonathan for his insights on working with groups in many cultures. He's personally taken Playback Theatre into twenty countries. At the summer-intensive courses in the School of Playback Theatre, he leads diverse groups. People come from around the world. They have widely varying backgrounds and beliefs. And they bring all levels of experience with Playback Theatre. We've included the transcript of the interview here.

Q: Jonathan, you've worked all over the world, often in cultures very different from your own. What makes you successful at connecting with people who differ from you?

J.F.: Being interested in different cultures. If you are resistant to adapting how you might work in your own country, you won't be successful.

You have to be willing to work in the unknown. You will encounter unexpected responses, and to welcome the unexpected is important. For example, you plan to have a discussion in the group. You ask a question, and nobody answers. You can't figure out why everyone is being so quiet, when in the States individuals would want to express themselves. You find the mindset is very different.

I was working in Japan when in the middle of the session a participant said he had to leave. I asked why. He said he felt discouraged. I said, "It's okay, you can stay." He said no, he had to leave. It turned out he didn't want to bring the rest of the group down with his feeling. Japanese will feel they have to remove themselves so they don't negatively impact the group. In the U.S., that individual might complain that you are not satisfying him or her with your training—he or she was expecting something different. It was a different response, very unexpected to me. I persuaded the person to talk about his feeling publicly in the group. What he had to say was relevant to our training and everybody there.

Another factor, perhaps, is a kind of humility, to be open and welcoming to whatever may come your way and ready to roll it in, to accept offers and not reject them because they are strange or you don't understand them. Someone gives you an offer, and you really don't quite understand it. You're the trainer, the authority. It would be easy to reject it. But if you have the humility to consider it, from *anybody*, you may, in fact, learn something by accepting it that you would not learn if you rejected it.

Q: When you enter a new culture, you do that with a set of assumptions about what you will find there. What are some of the assumptions that help you?

J.F.: I count on the fundamental humanity of anyone, anywhere. With big cultural differences, we often can feel that someone else isn't fully human. You have to go through certain layers of prejudice and resistance in yourself to truly believe that everyone has hopes and fears and daily struggles and hearts that can be full and eyes that can be wet. And if you really believe this in your interaction with people, they sense it and will open to you. It's not easy.

The first time I went to Africa, I was working under very crude conditions with people who seemed undereducated and of a culture so foreign to me that I could feel the pull to retreat into a kind of professional isolation, to do my teaching and go back to my hotel, as opposed to challenging myself to be open to the humanity of each one of these strange people.

Q: What did you do when you realized that?

J.F.: The breaks, the pauses are important for finding different ways to be in relationship with individual participants informally. It's pushing through the resistance to be in contact and get to know people.

With different people, you hang out in different ways. With one, you have a discussion. With another, you don't know the same language, but you might pour them tea or just stand next to them smiling.

I may try and fail with some people, especially if the person is isolated in some way. You look her in the eye, smile, and stand close to her.

Q: If you had to coach me to connect with someone I'd never met who came from a different culture, what would you tell me to do?

J.F.: First, I would coach you on a few words of the language. You're going to get incredible mileage from these few words, because people will know that you have the interest and have gone to the trouble to take a few steps across the bridge to them. Even if it's just "Thank you" and "Good morning."

Next, I would teach a little bit about how to pick up on cues about communication styles. For example, in Asia, people often might stand side by side while talking and look at each other through peripheral vision, not face to face and eye to eye as we would in the U.S. Or the way people use their hands when talking in Italy. I'd give you some feel of what it's like to express yourself in the same way, so expressively.

I'd suggest that you discover a little about how people are used to learning something and how it might differ from expectations in the U.S. Many cultures are used to a very authoritarian, hierarchical style of instruction. If you come in too friendly and egalitarian, they will be extremely uncomfortable. You have to at least be aware of that and start by giving them the structure they expect or you easily can make big mistakes. If they don't get a certain level of formality at the beginning, they won't respect you. You fulfill that expectation and then lead them to a looser style.

I'd remind you that you will learn as you go along. If you're open to what you're seeing and experiencing and learning from it as you go along, the group will teach you how to teach them.

I expect to feel clumsy when I enter a new culture. My normal feeling of myself as a highly experienced practitioner has to be suspended in the beginning. I have learned to be patient with myself and recognize that it takes some time to learn to read the cues, to learn what I need to learn to make the training truly successful in a profound way.

You will benefit from the capacity to take in information while you're delivering, to do both at the same time. People have widely varying abilities to do this, to be speaking, lecturing, putting out at the same time as taking in and processing information. You're noticing how people are sitting, and it informs your next sentence or little segment. We're always doing two things at once, like the

circular breathing someone has to use when playing the didger-
idoo.

Q: It's like in African dancing and drumming, where you never
know if it's the drummers who are driving the dancers or the
dancers who are influencing the pace of the drumming.

J.F.: That's right. It's very cybernetic. If you have too hierarchical
a view of your role as an expert or a teacher, it won't work. It will
get in the way of taking in information at every second.

You walk into a room ostensibly to give a lecture, but from the
moment you walk in, you have the attitude "What can I learn
here? What will make this work?" You totally have the antennae
out to learn in lots of different ways, from body cues, from what
they say and what they don't, how they interact and don't, from
how they position themselves in the room in relation to you and to
each other.

Q: What do you do when you have great diversity among the
group members to help them cohere and use diversity to advantage?

J.F.: One thing I always do is to give space for each person to be
seen and heard in the group, through introductions or whatever
way. I prefer not to work in groups that are so large that you can't
do that.

I often do social mapping according to identifiable subsets of
the group, such as where you come from, or how much experience
you have with the subject at hand. There are two purposes for
social mapping: the first is to name the differences so it's easier to
return to them if you need to in later discussion. If you have
twenty-eight men and seven women, doing social mapping on
those criteria allows you later to come back to the subject of men

and women if you need to. The second purpose is to help isolated individuals be more comfortable and feel included. For example, "Who's had more or less experience with this subject?" allows you to discover someone at the far end of the line who's had very little experience. You as the teacher then can say, "This course is for everybody, including you there. No matter how much you already know or don't know, there's something for you to gain here." It takes a kind of tact, but the purpose is to help people feel that it's okay to be there. Using that method is a kind of preventative.

It's also helpful to have methods to deal with conflict when it arises. Conflict can often lead to tremendous learning. There are some differences you can deal with in a group, whatever the context, and some you can't because it's not appropriate or constructive. The leader must decide what's feasible and what isn't.

We each have our style and strengths as leaders. Some are much better at a confrontational style; others have a gentle style tending toward harmony. What's important as leaders is the flexibility to confront conflict on one hand and promote harmony on the other. You have to know when to do what within your own style.

CHAPTER 5 AT A GLANCE

Leading groups in other cultures and facilitating diverse gatherings can be uncomfortable at first. Establishing rapport and helping the group members to connect requires special attention to cultural differences and cues. It can help to follow these suggestions:

- Do your homework about participants and their cultures. Take plenty of time to plan your first three minutes.

- The meaning of cues varies from culture to culture. Be patient. Experiment and adjust.
- Tune in to your own reactions and change them if they're not productive.
- Expect to feel a little clumsy at first.
- Let the group members know you want to learn about their cultures.
- Use techniques like social mapping to acknowledge and celebrate a group's diversity.

CHAPTER 6

TWENTY QUESTIONS

O ne of our favorite things about speaking and consulting is the conversations we have with individuals from all walks of life about the challenges they're facing. Occasionally, someone presents such an issue in a group. More often, somebody pulls us aside on a break or waits until everyone else has left after a speech. In quiet voices, they tell us about problems they're having connecting, hoping maybe we can help.

Moments like these are our best openings for making a difference in the world. Sometimes all we really need to do is listen. Other times, we ask questions, usually to help the person clarify the situation. Sometimes we give advice. The situations presented offer us opportunities to test the principles and practices we preach and to apply them in a variety of industries.

In this chapter, we've captured twenty of the questions we've been asked in recent years. Each presents an interesting scenario that allows us to drill deeper into the core principles and pathways. They come from all over the world. Some are unique, some commonplace. Some are major problems, others just minor irritants. All have to do with closing the gap when people are different. We responded individually to demonstrate options and to provide more multidimensional answers.

Q. 1: Working with Eskimos in Prudhoe Bay north of the Arctic Circle, I often feel like they don't give my suggestions the same weight as those from their fellow Eskimos. What kind of bridge do I build when it seems my credibility is marginal?

Claire responds: You certainly are working in a fascinating place with interesting challenges. Establishing credibility there may be quite different from establishing credibility elsewhere. For example, in some places, an engineer, welder, or surveyor is considered credible on the basis of experience, degrees, and certifications. This may not be the case with Eskimo workers in Alaska, who come from unique cultures. Many of them support drilling but simultaneously worry about the future of their homeland, one of the last untouched wilderness areas in the world. Establishing your credibility may take time.

Your Eskimo coworkers will reveal the answers to your question. Be respectfully curious about the individuals you work with. Learn all you can about them, the cultures they come from, how decisions are made, and how credibility is granted. Be interested because you will learn and benefit. Don't expect reciprocity or be disappointed if your interest isn't reciprocated.

Identify those whose suggestions are given merit. Watch and listen to the way suggestions are given and received. These are the cues you need. Then experiment, try giving suggestions in a similar way. Notice the responses you get. Be patient. Experiment and adjust.

Lara responds: It's certainly possible that your coworkers' response to you is based on a cultural bias on their part. It's also possible that there's another reason that they are slow to adopt your suggestions. At this stage, you don't know what's motivating their behavior. Engage your curiosity. Treat this situation as a mystery. You have one working assumption now: "My credibility is marginal with them because I'm not an Eskimo." What are the other possibilities? Could it be something you're *doing* that undermines your credibility? If you were an anthropologist, what would you see from third-person perspective? Form another working assumption based on the careful observation Claire suggests. Experiment and adjust from there.

Q. 2: My corporation recently acquired a manufacturing plant in Melbourne, Australia, which I've visited twice. My counterpart seems to be a good-time guy who's always telling me jokes and wants to take me to lunch at the pub for several beers. I'm not a stiff or a workaholic, but I don't drink during business hours. How can I handle this?

Lara responds: It sounds like you want to maintain a good relationship with your new colleague, but not at the cost of violating your standards for conduct during working hours. For the purpose of connecting, it may help you to focus more on his intentions than on his behavior. Let him know you enjoy his company and his humor by continuing to respond to his jokes with a good laugh. Then find a moment when the connection seems good to say something like, "I appreciate the way you've taken me under your wing. You've gone out of your way to make me feel a part of things here. Unfortunately, I don't function so well in the afternoons when I've been drinking. I hope that won't get in the way."

If that sounds too direct, pick up on cues in the style of his humor, and deliver your message in a similar style. For example, if he tends toward the irreverent, bantering style that many Aussie men use with each other, deliver your message that way.

Claire responds: How about suggesting that you meet for a beer at the pub *after* work? It will give you an opportunity to establish a friendly connection without violating your personal standards.

Q. 3: Some of the people that you mention in your book can read subtle cues. They see things that others might miss. How can I increase my ability to observe small changes in a person's behavior?

Claire responds: That you want to get better at reading cues is important; it means you're focusing on cues. That alone will cause improvement. There are all kinds of cues to tune in to—voice (volume, pace, tone), facial expressions, gestures, dress, surroundings. Cues vary from person to person; a raised eyebrow may mean one thing from one person and something entirely different from another. And what a shrug signals from someone on Tuesday may signal something different on Friday, so cues need to be evaluated in context.

Don't try to take on too many at once. Begin by focusing on reading one type of cue. You might want to choose one of the more obvious—like facial expressions—and focus on it for a day or a week. Then work on another type of cue. With practice, you can become masterful at reading people.

Lara responds: The best way to improve your ability to read people is to break it down so you can observe one kind of cue at a time. For example, you might begin by paying attention to changes in skin color for a day or two. Watch for occasions when someone blushes or goes pale. Then think about what might have triggered the change—play the last few moments of the conversation back, and see if you can identify the trigger. Do the same thing with the following cues:

- Eyes widening and narrowing
- Pupils dilating
- Eyebrows rising or knitting
- Nostrils flaring

- Head tilting
- Head nodding and shaking side to side
- Pen tapping

You'll want to pay attention to the physical signs that indicate when someone's state of mind shifts. You'll find it easier to do this by beginning with obvious shifts: a strong state of embarrassment or irritation, for example. Once you're able to read blatant changes, you can pay even closer attention to pick up more subtle changes.

Q. 4: I have several crews of landscapers. Most are Mexican and don't speak much English. I speak about a hundred words of Spanish. What kind of bridge can I build with a hundred words?

Lara responds: Your hundred words can take you quite a ways across the gap. Let your crews know that you want to improve your Spanish, and use lots of nonverbal matching and mirroring to enlarge your "vocabulary" beyond the verbal side of the communication. Ask for their help as you improve your language skills, and be receptive to their input. As they see you step out of your comfort zone to reach out, they are likely to do their part to meet you in the middle. Your vocabulary already includes words like "por favor" and "gracias," no doubt. Using them frequently will clearly communicate your intention to connect.

Technology can help you, too. There are portable electronic translators available these days. You type in a word or phrase, and the device translates it into Spanish on the spot.

Claire responds: That's a great start—one hundred words. I like Lara's suggestions, and I think you and your crew can have a lot of fun together learning to be bilingual in the language of landscaping. If you decide against a portable electronic translator, you might consider making a comprehensive list of basic landscaping terms in both languages, including names for tools, structures, and plants along with verbs that describe the actions involved. Make copies for everyone. You probably already know how to pronounce the terms and how to conjugate the verbs. With the list in everybody's pockets, you can give directions in both English and Spanish and, with some coaching from your crew, everyone will get an on-the-spot language lesson.

You might also gather the crew around the truck first thing in the morning or at the start of each new project phase to go over the work assignments. Use gestures and some of those hundred words—sort of like you would in charades—to elicit as much Spanish from the crew as possible for your language lesson. Then practice your new phrases and words as you have the crew repeat the English equivalents for their lesson.

Q. 5: I've been physically active all my life, including college and the U.S. Army. My new wife has three kids from her first marriage, but they just want to read and play computer games. They're sadly out of shape, and I can't motivate them. What do I do?

Claire responds: To establish a connection with these kids, build on your similarities first. Do you also enjoy reading? You might read a book—or one in the same genre—that one of them is reading and talk about it together. Or find a computer game to play with one of them. Watch a favorite TV show with them. Get to know them better by participating in their world. Eventually, you might invite them to watch an outdoor program or the Discovery channel, or you can suggest a book that might get them interested in a sport or other activity.

Once you establish a bond, invite one of them to do something active with you. Start with something that appeals to them. Remember that what appeals to one may not appeal to another.

Most important, remember that it's impossible to motivate someone else. Getting in shape is each individual's choice and responsibility. Can you accept them the way they are?

Lara responds: What is your intention? Is it to connect with the kids? Or to change them? If your intention is to change them, what will that do for you? It might be good to notice your own reactions first. Do you feel that their physical conditioning reflects on you or embarrasses you?

Kids usually pick up on judgment in adults, especially in authority figures. Begin by getting to know them. What motivates them? What do they get out of reading and computer games? Find out about that—it may give you some clues about what *might* motivate an interest in fitness. Once you've learned enough about each one (each individual is a culture) to build a strong second-person perspective, you can step into their shoes.

Then the question is "How do I get from *here* [their perspective] to *there* [a genuine interest in fitness]?" You will probably be most successful if your strategy rewards tiny steps toward the goal and if you evaluate your own progress on the basis of how successfully you connect with each child. You'll know you've really connected when you find yourself being influenced by them, as well.

Q. 6: After serving in the Marine Corps in Vietnam, I came home distrusting Orientals. Now I'm working with Vietnamese, Cambodians, and Laotians. How can I learn to trust them after all these years?

Lara responds: You've already taken the most important step: noticing your reaction, realizing that it's based on powerful experiences from your past but that are now outdated and irrelevant to your current situation. Maybe the next step is not to expect yourself to trust or distrust Asians as a group but to learn about each individual as a culture. Everybody is trustworthy in some areas, and less trustworthy in others. One way to overcome such a limiting belief is to learn about each person and his or her unique history and the perspective he or she has gained as a result. Gaining a rich understanding of the person tends to make the category ("Oriental" or "Asian") fade into the background as you come to appreciate what's unique and admirable, flawed and human, in this particular case. The challenge is to find out enough to enable you to decide what to trust and distrust based on a true understanding of the person with whom you are dealing.

Claire responds: Your honest appraisal is an excellent start. That you want to change says a lot about the kind of person you are. It sounds like you are currently thinking of these people in a category that describes race and ethnicity. Would it be possible to begin to think of them in other categories as well? As work partners? As neighbors? As team members?

You are clear in your first-person perspective. Why not step into second-person perspective, view things from the point of view of one of the people you're struggling to trust? How might that other person see the world today? How might that person view you? How might he or she see the project you're working on? When you find you can stay in the other person's skin long enough to describe yourself and your work project without stepping back over into your own perspective, you will have a clear second-person perspective for this situation. Then, you might step into third-person perspective to watch a future interaction. Talk to yourself as a coach about ways to change the way you react.

Q. 7: Last month I was given a team of nine computer programmers to manage. I have no background in the sciences or computers. Half the time I don't understand their challenges and accomplishments. It's literally a different language. Can you help?

Claire responds: Begin to connect with these computer programmers by learning the language necessary to discuss the big picture, goals, and major challenges. Is there one of them who might be able to teach you the basics? It's possible that all of them might enjoy sitting down to brief you. As you continue to work with them, stay curious. Be a learner. Take a class or find a mentor.

It's not a common business practice to put someone in charge of computer programmers who has no background in computer programming, but you were put in charge for a reason. My hunch is that you're a good manager. This may be your strongest connection with the group. Everyone loves a great manager—someone who has their best interests in mind, who will help them and their projects make their way through the politics of the organization, who will run interference for them, who will be an advocate.

Tell them what you need and turn them loose to do their work, and be open to their input.

Lara responds: You might start by asking each of them to tell you about what's important to them in their work, questions like "What accomplishments are you most proud of?" and then following the question with further genuine interest with questions like, "And because I'm in the process of getting familiar with the technical side—so I can really understand what a difference that made—what was the benefit to the company?" You're in a situation in which a little self-deprecating humor, balanced with a strong sense of the value you bring to the job, can go a long way to helping you meet them in the middle of the work you're doing together.

Q. 8: My boss is fair, honest, helpful, and even-handed. The problem is I find her remote and a bit standoffish. In many ways she's the best supervisor I've ever had, but she talks about little except work. How can I find out who she is outside of work?

Lara responds: It's great that you can make the distinction between her management skills and the distance you feel from her as a person. The place to start is in the realization that although you may never know what they are, there are good reasons for her remoteness. It's probably best to expect that if she warms up at all, she will do so slowly. If you are willing to respect her need for distance and at the same time watch and listen for signs and cues of openness to getting to know one another, she may become more approachable with time. Pushing for familiarity before she demonstrates that she's ready for it would probably increase her reserve.

You also can try making some offers and noticing her responses. For example, if she doesn't already know how much you appreciate that she's "fair, honest, helpful, and even-handed," you might tell her so. Or you could make an offer in very general terms, to avoid putting pressure on her, to open up. Try something like "It really helps me to get to know the people I work with as people." Her response to either of those offers will tell you a lot about her level of receptiveness to a warmer affiliation.

Claire responds: It sounds like you have an excellent work relationship. I'm wondering if there's something you want from it that you're not getting. In the past, have your bosses given you a lot of praise and reinforcement? If so, you may need to change your expectations and get those needs met elsewhere. Get clear on your intent—what you really need from her.

Her remoteness and standoffishness may be cues that she wants to keep things where they are. If you try too hard to find out who she is outside the job—and keep in mind she may not *have* much of a life beyond work—it may seem intrusive.

If you think through all of this and decide you still want to get to know her better personally, take note of other cues and hints. Is there a picture of a son or daughter on her desk? Or a photo of her sailing? Or does she wear a ski jacket in the winter? These are all possible openings.

Q. 9: Providing inner-city teens with wilderness adventures has been challenging. The adventure part is easy enough: they learn teamwork pretty quickly. But I can tell that most of them don't really relate to me. I'm British and don't speak the way they do, and I don't listen to the same kind of music. What can I do to connect with them?

Claire responds: I'd recommend you use what you already have— teamwork and wilderness adventure. Strengthen and build that connection. Lots of adults are mystified by teenagers—even those from their own country. That you are British probably isn't perceived as a gap by the youth you're working with. Teenagers tend to be attracted to differences. Play off of your foreignness rather than trying to fit in. Teens usually don't like adults who try to blend in with them. Be their role model and leader, not their buddy.

Meanwhile, turn the spotlight on them. Be curious about them. Ask them to teach you about their music and the terms they use— not because you're trying to be one of them but because you're genuinely interested in learning from and about them.

Lara responds: Capitalize on their curiosity about you. Teens pay more attention to what adults *do* than to what we say. They tend to be strongly attracted to those who are secure in their own identity. They can smell it a mile away when we need their approval. Do engage your curiosity about them. And also be aware that it's sometimes more effective with teens to leave a bit of gap between you for *them* to traverse. In other words, let them come to you. Be prepared to meet them when they do. One of the best ways to do that is to ask them about their opinions and insights in a respectful way. They are deep in the process of forming their views, and being able to express them to an adult who listens without judging helps them in their development. Sometimes it helps to pay more attention to the developmental task they face—building their skills in evaluation and sound judgment—than to the opinions they are trying out as part of mastering the task.

Q. 10: Sometimes I get so nervous around people with different backgrounds that I become awkward and can't form understandable sentences. I "freeze up" and sometimes stammer. How can I relax and relate to them as if I were with friends and family?

Lara responds: It sounds like you get self-conscious, and it builds on itself as you feel awkward. The solution to this problem can be found in opening up your curiosity. As long as you focus your attention on yourself and your own "performance" around people who are different, the awkwardness and anxiety will grow. When you can turn your attention outside yourself, toward the people you are getting to know, you'll relax and be able to enjoy them.

One way to start is to think about one or two things you'd like to know about them as people. For example, what can you learn from the differences in their backgrounds? Or, given that people from different backgrounds have sometimes been through radical transitions in their lives, moving from one continent and culture to another, for instance, you might ask them what that was like for them. What do they miss about their former home? What have they discovered here that's enriched them? What resources did they have to develop to make the change successfully? As long as your inquiry comes from a genuine interest in the other person, he or she will be happy to tell you about it. And while you are listening to others, the focus is on them and not on you. Curiosity helps you loosen up and relax by directing your attention to learning rather than critiquing your "performance."

Claire responds: Start by clarifying your intent, and have it be one that focuses on "the other." For example, your intent might be to make others feel comfortable and relaxed. That will shift the spotlight from your awkwardness to the responses of those you're interacting with.

Use this book as your guide. As you meet people from other backgrounds, choose a principle, pathway, or perspective to focus on. And be patient with yourself. It's natural to feel awkward. Rarely do we feel as if we're with friends and family when we first meet someone, especially when we're from different backgrounds.

Q. 11: Recently I was sent from our New Jersey corporate offices to rural Mississippi to settle a dispute between two of our subsidiaries. My feedback from day one was, "Slow down, you'll get more done." I know I'm a hard charger, but I feel like the Southerners are dragging their feet. Help!

Claire responds: "Slow down, you'll get more done," is a cue on a silver platter. You'd be foolish not to heed it. You are likely to get the dispute settled more efficiently and effectively by conforming to the Mississippians' druthers. Take a breath after someone says something and before you respond. When speaking, slow down. Pause between thoughts. Think of it as slowing down to get ahead!

Once you've matched the pace of the people you're working with long enough for them to feel comfortable with you, you can begin to pick up speed and bring them along with you. Watch for cues to know that it's working.

When you're working on your own, you can work at your own fast pace. Just be sure to show them where you are on the master plan so they can follow along and see that you're efficient—not rushed.

Lara responds: The advice you got from your coworkers was good but incomplete. You are in a new culture. It's not that things don't get done in Mississippi; it's just that people build a personal context before they get down to business. Sit down with someone who knows and loves the culture there. Ask, "What do I have to learn from the culture here? How will I get better when I learn it?"

Open your eyes and ears to pick up on cultural cues as if you were in Bombay or Buenos Aires. How do the people here build rapport with each other? What do they do? How do they know when it's time to move from rapport building to getting down to business?

Match their voice tempo and tone as a way of building rapport. Listen carefully to the rhythm and pace of someone's speech and just let yourself fall into the same rhythm. Don't go so far as to change your accent—that could break rapport if the person feels imitated or mocked. Just match the tempo. Notice what happens to the rapport between you. Also take note of what happens in your body when you do that, especially to your level of tension or relaxation. Watch out: when you get into the rhythm, Mississippi may get into you.

Q. 12: I'm in charge of a university tutoring program where students can get help from upperclassmen. One of our honors calculus majors, a man from Thailand, is a tutor who gives me lots of hours. But students complain to me that he talks too fast and that his pronunciation is difficult to understand.

Lara responds: Is he aware of the students' feedback? Perhaps you can coach him and his students to develop feedback systems. In the short term, he needs better methods for checking whether they understand him. Although it may seem crude, one option would be to suggest that he ask his students to use a simple signal to indicate whether they understand him or not, for example, pausing often for a check: thumbs up, "I get it," thumbs down, "I don't get it," thumbs sideways, "I'm not sure I get it."

In the long term, he needs to learn to watch for subtler cues. The short-term strategy gives him clear signals. Suggest that he build his ability to read people by combining the thumb signals with reading the student's facial expression and voice tone for comprehension. It may even help for you to "shadow" him for a few tutoring sessions, interpreting nonverbal cues for him until he's able to read them independently of you.

Claire responds: I'd get your tutor actively involved in the solution. If you try to figure this out for him, you miss out on his insights and he misses a learning opportunity.

Assure him that you are pleased with his work and appreciate all the hours he gives you. Then lay the problem out for him and ask him for his ideas about how to solve it. Discuss with him the possibility of working with an English as a Second Language (ESL) instructor who has experience with the unique pronunciation difficulties that Thai speakers encounter with English. Are there a couple of students—ones who wouldn't be threatening to him—who could get involved in the solution? Tell him you're willing to sit in on a session or two if he thinks it would be helpful.

Q. 13: One of my colleagues is Muslim, so he has different beliefs than I do about the role of women. He and I are equals on our work team, but I'm the only woman and he tells me what to do. The other day he even patted me on the head as he patiently explained that it's important to respond to customers in a timely manner. He treats me like an idiot. I want to address this before I start to hate him.

Claire responds: Be careful about the assumptions you make. Your colleague's actions may be unrelated to his religion. Many Muslims view men and women as equals. You might be surprised to find that he treats you the way he does because you remind him of his daughter, or because he assumed you wanted reassurance, or for some other reason. It would be worthwhile to find out what patting someone on the head means to him; perhaps it means something entirely different to him than it does to you.

At the same time, your frustration is valid; I would feel insulted, too. Your reactions to his behavior could get in the way of your job effectiveness and satisfaction. I recommend spending a lot of time in third-person perspective with this man. That will help separate you from your anger and frustration so you can evaluate the situation more logically.

Then you'll need to experiment and adjust. From a third-person perspective, coach yourself through interactions with him. You might try patting him on the head. Then notice how effective or ineffective that action is in changing his behavior. Or coach yourself to sit down and talk openly with him. Tell him what your intent is—probably to work together effectively and for you both to feel respected and respectful. Tell him his orders and gestures are demeaning. Suggest other ways for him to communicate with you. Once again, notice his behavior and adjust. Continue experimenting and adjusting as you work to build a satisfying work relationship.

Lara responds: If you choose to sit down with him and talk openly, it will probably help to begin by framing your conversation carefully. You might open the conversation with, "I'm sure you don't intend to communicate disrespect, but that's the message I receive when you pat me on the head or tell me how important it is to get back to customers quickly. Would you be interested to know how I'd prefer you work with me?" Getting his permission to give him feedback may help him to be receptive to what you have to say.

Q. 14: I've lived and worked with black people most of my career. One guy I manage has tried several times to make me feel guilty for slavery and other injustices done to blacks. I have absolutely no "white guilt." What do I do?

Lara responds: That depends a lot on what you want to accomplish. Start with clarifying your intention. If your intention is to build a bridge, the first step is probably to engage your spirit of inquiry to find out more about how he thinks about the issue and develop a strong second-person perspective with him. Ask him if he's willing to share his point of view, then find out where his viewpoint came from with questions like "What experiences have you had that formed your opinion on this?"; "Have there been people in your life who were influential in bringing you to this perspective?"; and "Are there books or speeches that have been important to you?" Acknowledge and validate his answers to your questions. Doing this doesn't mean that you have to *agree* with his point of view, only that you express understanding and appreciate what it means to him. For example, you might say, "Okay, I understand how you see it," or "It makes sense that you'd come to that conclusion on the basis of your experiences."

Be sure that you can engage in the conversation from an open and nonjudgmental state of mind. If there are traces of self-righteousness or negative judgments of his views in your attitude as you have the conversation, he will sense it immediately, and you risk damaging the connection between you. To the extent that you can ask him about it "cleanly," with an open mind and sincere desire to hear him out, you will likely find out much more about him and his perspective. Third-person perspective can be helpful here. If you decide ahead of time that you'll step back at critical moments in the conversation, especially when you would be likely to "get hooked" or take his statements personally, it can help you to listen without judgment.

Here's where clarifying your intention in advance is most important. If your real intention is to show him how muddleheaded he is on this topic, it will be obvious in the way you frame the conversation. That's a recipe for relationship disaster. Starting a conversation with that intention won't help you to relate to him better.

Of course, you'll want to be sensitive to his responses to your questions. If he seems defensive, you may be asking too many questions in succession; that might be a cue that it's time to give the topic a break for a while and take it up another time.

Claire responds: I can't add much more without knowing what you want in this situation. Do you want this guy to leave you alone? Do you want him to quit talking about this topic? Do you want to show him you empathize but don't feel responsible?

Do you know what he wants? Getting clear on both intents—his and yours—might be the best place to start.

Q. 15: I have a staff of nine. Three of them often speak their native language to each other. Some of the others have come to my office and complained.

Claire responds: This situation offers a rich opportunity for your staff to learn from their differences. "The most creative teams," says Michael West, professor at Aston Business School, "are drawn from diverse backgrounds."[1] Such teams can solve problems creatively because of their varied perspectives. But diverse teams need to be managed well so that their differences remain constructive.

Each person on your staff is a rich source for information and insights. How about talking this issue through with all of them?

Ask the nonnative speakers when and why they tend to use their native language at work. Are they speaking their native language because they aren't fluent in English? Many people don't understand how difficult and time-consuming it is to learn a second language and, therefore, hold unrealistic expectations for how quickly their nonnative colleagues should become fluent. On the other hand, they may be using their native language because it would seem unnatural for them to speak English to each other. Talk openly about their decision to speak their native language among themselves to build understanding. Find out if there are limitations and barriers that keep them from speaking the common language.

Ask those who are uncomfortable with the nonnative language what, specifically, troubles them? Do they feel excluded when they can't understand conversation? Are they afraid the nonnative speakers are talking about them?

Then ask the group for ideas about how to solve this problem, if it is indeed a problem. Involving everyone greatly increases your odds for a successful outcome. As the leader, it would be great for you to facilitate some interactive activities so that they could have fun and learn about some of the other differences and similarities—beyond language—that exist in the group.

Lara responds: Meet with them. Start with describing the situation from your best second-person perspective. "It's great that you have the language in common, that you can speak easily with each other. When the three of you are alone, that works really well. When you're with other team members, though, they sometimes feel left out. You can imagine what it would be like for them; they can't understand or participate in your conversation. I know you want to be part of building a cohesive work team. Do you think you can see your way clear to speaking English when other team members are present?" Listen to their response carefully. There may be other reasons they use their language, rather than English. Be prepared to problem-solve further.

Q. 16: I'm a pharmaceutical rep. I make presentations to groups of doctors on a regular basis. The Titanium Rule seems like a great idea, but how would I apply it to a roomful of different people?

Lara responds: The best way to apply the Titanium Rule in a group situation is to find out what druthers the group might have in common, and then experiment and adjust by aiming your presentation to meet their needs, noticing their response, and adjusting accordingly. So in the specific case of presenting to doctors, you might start with a couple of working assumptions about their druthers.

Medical training attracts people with a bent for analytical, rational, and quantifiable data based on well-conducted empirical research. Given that they share that experience, belief system, and thinking style, they probably will prefer that you present your information in the same way.

Time is precious to physicians these days. With managed care pressuring them to reduce charges, they have to see more patients for more procedures a day to maintain revenue at the level they're accustomed to. They will appreciate a streamlined, just-the-essential-facts approach. You can leave time for follow-up questions after the presentation for those wanting to know more.

Claire responds: Lara has done a great job of laying out a set of working assumptions about doctors' druthers. I would add a couple more that have to do with pharmaceuticals. Most physicians will want to know where the various insurance providers stand on your product—is it on the *approved* list? And they will be interested in getting all the information available about legalities; let's face it, doctors are worried about lawsuits these days. There are probably other druthers you know about that you can add to the list—and you can constantly be learning about new ones.

Applying the Titanium Rule to a roomful of different people

can be challenging—but every bit as important as applying it one-on-one. Lara mentioned what is probably the best approach: making some working generalizations about the group and appealing to them.

A couple of other possibilities come to mind. One is to identify the one or two most influential people in the group—the key decision makers—and to adapt to their preferences. The other is to cover all your bases. If some are more analytical, others more imaginative, and some prefer things to be explained in detail while others like to get the big picture, you adapt your style by doing all these things, something for everyone.

Q. 17: I'm an Asian-American female working on a project with four other engineers, all male. When we get together to talk about the project, they are out of control. They talk loud, interrupt, insult each other—and then laugh, and they argue every point that's made. I know I'm every bit as technically competent as they are, but in these meetings I get quiet and withdraw. Their bravado makes me uncomfortable, and I feel excluded. How can I get them to quiet down and listen to me?

Lara responds: I doubt that you're going to have much success in taming those rowdy guys. It sounds like their boisterous style is driving you nuts. Your question assumes that the solution is for them to change and become more like you. That would bridge the gap. On the other hand, you would probably resent it if they insisted that this relationship would be just fine if only you would be just like them.

Your question made me think of the complexity of a piece of music by Bach. There's something compelling in listening to a piece in which one section of the orchestra is playing a rapid, rousing almost frenetic theme, and another instrument is laying down a simple, smoothly rhythmic counterpoint to the animated theme.

The parts are distinct and yet complement one another harmonically. What would it be like if you didn't have to match their style or demand that they match yours but found a way to weave your quiet, Asian presence into the madness? Timing is everything. You have a lot to offer them. Decide to include yourself, honoring your style, honoring theirs, and you'll find a way to blend them into something greater than the sum of the parts.

Claire responds: I asked my friend Pat Heim for her insights on your question. The author of *Hardball for Women*, *Smashing the Glass Ceiling*, and *In the Company of Women*, Pat is internationally recognized as an expert on gender issues in the workplace. She says men and women live in two different cultures. Her research shows that the male culture tends to be hierarchical, while the female culture is shared more equally—among girls there is never a boss doll player. "One of the ways men negotiate their place in the hierarchy," says Pat, "is through verbal bantering." That includes making fun of each other and putting each other down. It's a form of bonding for men. "These differences are a double whammy for you," she says, "because the Asian cultures are often more subdued and not as raucous as Western cultures."

Pat recommends three possible responses. One is to say to yourself, "This behavior looks rude to me, but it's just the way these guys bond and have fun. It's not about me." Another response follows our Titanium Rule—do unto others according to their druthers. In this case, you would adapt your style to "fit in" with the team. You would be rowdier. The downside to this approach is that it can be exhausting to constantly do what is uncomfortable for you. Pat's third suggestion is to consider training on gender differences for the group. This could be done via a video, DVD, or workshop. Training about this issue would give all of you some new models which might make it more comfortable to talk about the bantering and your discomfort with it. "The most important thing to keep in mind," says Pat, "is that none of you are wrong—just different."

Q. 18: I'm one of the pastors at a suburban, mostly white church. We are in the process of "adopting" three families, refugees of Hurricane Katrina. All are African American. I have three coordinators, senior members of the church, who will work directly with each family. Their role will be to get to know the families and to work with our church community to find homes, schools, jobs, clothing, and furniture to meet their needs. These three members volunteered for the role, so I know they have big hearts, but I'm not sure they have the interpersonal skills they need to interact with families from such different backgrounds. I just have a couple of hours with the three of them in my office before they get started. What should I try to teach them?

Claire responds: First, kudos to the church and all of you for your generosity in adopting survivors of Hurricane Katrina. Such efforts rekindle our faith in each other. Certainly, you will make a huge difference in the lives of the survivors, but I think you will be amazed at the difference they will make in your lives as well. This project offers a wealth of learning and enrichment.

I would begin the session with your three coordinators with two *don'ts:* don't expect reciprocity, and don't impose your values and needs on the families. The coordinators need to begin their work with *no strings attached.* Most likely, the family members will be grateful beyond measure, but they may not *show* their gratitude in the way the coordinators would expect. The way we demonstrate appreciation varies from culture to culture. The families likely have been traumatized, and the coordinators may find them challenging to work with at times. If the coordinators go into the project expecting positive reinforcement, they may be disappointed. You can assist by helping them set up realistic expectations and by staying in touch over the coming weeks and months. Perhaps you will be the one who pats them on the back and acknowledges them for the work they're doing.

I would also help them to understand how important it is that *they not impose their own needs and values.* Each coordinator has his or her assumptions about what the families want and need. Typically, we ask ourselves, "If I had lost my home and everything in it, what would I need now?" If the coordinators use their own answers to guide their actions, it's Golden Rule thinking. I might assume that getting school clothes for a child would be a first priority—because that's the way I would feel in similar circumstances. But I might learn that finding a soccer team the child could join would be more important to her. Or I might plan to acquire material possessions for the family when what's really needed is emotional support. It will be important that the coordinators listen and observe and then listen some more to learn from each family member.

Now to the *do's.* In the meeting, I would ask the coordinators to *clarify their intention.* Ultimately, when the project has been completed, how do they want the families they're working with to think and feel about the relocation effort and the people involved? What do the coordinators want for themselves? What will success for this project look like?

I would talk to them about the importance of *noticing and valuing their own reactions as* things unfold. I might brainstorm with them what some of their possible reactions might be in the first week or two. They might feel empathetic, confused, overwhelmed, sad, frustrated, or impatient. They might even notice racist feelings they weren't aware of. What's important is to know that these are all natural, that it's important to be aware of them, and that when they notice reactions that aren't productive, they can change them.

To establish a bond, they will need to *find similarities* with each family member, things they have in common. If the families are members of the same denomination as you are, this might be a good place to start.

In that first meeting, I would help the coordinators understand how important it will be to *read cues*. When we rush in to help those who have suffered major tragedies, we tend to be all action. This is a time instead for listening, for observing, for learning about those who we want to help. In the first hours and days, the coordinators will learn who the family members are, who's in charge, what emotional state each is in, what kinds of things are important to each, what doesn't much matter. This information will be invaluable in meeting their needs.

Finally, I'd tell the coordinators to give themselves permission to *experiment and adjust*. In their shoes, we'd all be learners. They're going to try things that don't work. They're going to do things that work beautifully. They'll be learning as they go. They need to give themselves permission to try a number of different approaches.

Lara responds: Great suggestions, Claire. The only thing I'd add is that you can help your coordinators by teaching them to use lots of second-person perspective. You might start your orientation by asking your coordinators to imagine they are standing in the shoes of the evacuees. For example, you could say, "You've had to flee for your lives from a wall of water. You were trapped on a rooftop for hours waiting for help to arrive. You had to leave your dog behind, and you still don't know what happened to him. You have only the clothes on your back. Family photographs, mementos, the quilt your great-grandmother made, your children's art work, your bank records, are all gone. You've heard some people criticize people like you for not taking the hurricane evacuation warnings seriously. Once you left your home, you were shifted from place to place. Now you are being adopted by this church. What are you thinking and feeling? What do you need the most? What are some of the things you might not be able to say or ask for? What are your worst fears?"

Q. 19: I'm a college freshman. In one of my classes, we were assigned partners for a project that will account for 60 percent of our final grade. I got Amber. She's a sorority girl who seems to go to parties every night. We met for coffee last week to talk about our project and all she wanted to do was talk about the cute frat boy she met the night before. We didn't even decide what our topic is going to be. Instead, she kept trying to talk me into going to a party with her on the weekend. There's going to be a guy there she thinks I'd like. I'm gay, but I didn't tell her. I don't think it's any of her business. I want to do well this first semester. How can I get a good grade on this project with Amber as my partner?

Lara responds: You and Amber seem to have different intentions. You want to get a good grade and to preserve your privacy. She wants to have fun and connect with you by fixing you up with the frat boy. Even though her approach is pretty far off the mark for connecting with you, her intentions are good. You don't have to meet all of her expectations to get a connection going, and you certainly don't have to give her more information about you than you're comfortable with. You can, however, meet in the middle on her other intention. What would make the process of doing the project together fun for both of you? Let her know that you're prepared to be flexible in how you go about it. Offer up some creative approaches: rapid-fire brainstorming for a topic on the quad with the first three people walking by that you can persuade to join in, or posting a chart on a community wall with the title "Amber and _____'s Project. Free latte for best idea posted by October 12 at 2 P.M."

Be sure to let Amber know that it's important for you to get a good grade on the project. At the appropriate moment, tell her what you expect from her as a project partner in a tone that assumes the best. Then pay attention to how she participates. Be prepared to experiment and adjust.

Claire responds: I think Lara's suggestions for making the project more fun are great. And I agree that there's no need for you to discuss your sexual orientation with Amber. I have one other suggestion that uses the Titanium Rule. Since the sorority seems to mean a lot to Amber, you might talk about how important making good grades is to becoming an active member. Then good grades might be something you can work toward together.

Q. 20: We expect that the hotel we're building in Beijing will be filled with North Americans during the upcoming summer Olympics. Most of the people we are hiring have had little exposure to North Americans, although they have all passed a test of their English. We believe that people from Canada and the United States expect outgoing customer service, direct eye contact, and big, friendly smiles from everyone they meet in our hotel. Is that what we should teach our new hires?

Claire responds: I applaud you for thinking through this customer-service issue and planning appropriate training. You're correct in believing that most people from North America respond well to direct eye contact—and that they make assumptions when people don't look at them. I was in Beijing in May. At the end of the first day, when almost no one had made eye contact with me, I decided people didn't like me. When I noticed my nearly unconscious reaction, I reminded myself that in many Asian countries, direct eye contact is equated with staring. It is seen as intrusive, even threatening. Averting one's eyes, on the other hand, can be a sign of respect.

The most valuable skill you can teach your new employees is to observe gestures and other nonverbals and to match them in order to establish rapport with customers. Then they will be prepared to interact successfully with people from all over the world and from a variety of cultures. These matching skills will help them to be more effective in all areas of their lives for years to come.

Smiling is the one gesture that everyone can count on to bridge gaps. It is rarely misunderstood. Roger Axtell, expert on international business, tells us that scientists believe that smiling releases endorphins that create a sense of mild euphoria, so not only can a smile make a customer feel welcome, it may make an employee having a bad day feel a little better.[2] Encourage your employees to smile freely and often.

Lara responds: I agree with Claire's suggestions. Perhaps you can frame the challenge to your employees as taking the next step in mastering English. Each language has not only a verbal vocabulary but also a nonverbal vocabulary, accompanying nonverbal signals that indicate understanding, agreement, interest, and respect along with the literal meanings of what people say. Being able to enter a culture by speaking the nonverbal language along with the words and grammar greatly increases your chances of being not only heard but understood in that language.

CHAPTER 7

CROSSING THE BRIDGE—
THREE CASE STUDIES

Now it's your turn. We've chosen three scenarios for you to consider. One has to do with facilitating a training program for twenty-four people, all from different countries. Another is about an older worker and a new younger manager. The last concerns a creative executive who works with people she finds boring and analytical.

There are all kinds of differences here—racial and ethnic, educational, work style, generational, gender, religious, positional, and political. These case studies will give you an opportunity to immerse yourself in challenging real-life work situations that deal with differences. You will be able to step back from each scenario and analyze it by identifying differences, shifting perspective, clarifying intention, applying core principles, finding applications for the pathways, and making recommendations. Thoroughly deliberating these situations will help you to handle your own diversity challenges.

LYNN AND THE LINE MANAGERS

Lynn is ready to get to work. She slept off and on last night on the seventeen-hour flight that arrived midmorning in Hong Kong. After checking in to her hotel, she went downstairs to work out, then had lunch delivered to her room. Now she needs to do the last piece of planning for tomorrow. Lynn is a forty-something consultant with a training and consulting company that specializes in quality. She grew up in Montana and has traveled extensively, working with clients in Europe, Asia, and South America.

Lynn has come to Hong Kong to lead a six-day session for line managers who work with the Asian division of a Fortune 500 financial company. These twenty-four line managers will be the force in this part of the world behind a new company-wide quality initiative. Over the six days, they will learn everything there is to know about the initiative: where it came from, why it makes sense, how the details will get handled. And they will learn to facilitate sessions that teach employees at all levels—above and below them—the same information. The challenge they face goes beyond mastering content. Once they've completed their facilitation training, the line managers will return to their own countries and facilitate sessions in their own languages. In those sessions, they will also aim to transform attitudes and encourage each employee to step up to a higher level of leadership and accountability.

Lynn is not a stranger to the six-day session; she ran one just last week for the American division, so she knows how to put fledgling facilitators through their paces to master the training material. But she also knows that the first three minutes of tomorrow's session are crucial, and she hasn't decided yet quite how to handle those critical moments. The managers she'll be working with come from Pakistan, India, Japan, China, Korea, Thailand, Indonesia, Bangladesh, Taiwan, and the Philippines. All speak English fairly well, so language isn't a barrier. But Asia is more historically complex and culturally diverse than most other parts of the world, and these managers come from countries with vastly different cultures and politics. Some of the countries represented have been at odds for centuries.

Those first three minutes will make all the difference. This will be the time for her to connect and build credibility with the twenty-four people she'll be leading for the rest of the week.

1. What are some of the differences Lynn needs to bridge?

2. A good place for Lynn to start would be to clarify her intention for the first three minutes. What do you think she should try to accomplish?

3. Move into second-person perspective for a moment. Put yourself in the chair of one of the line managers. Lynn comes to the front of the room. What would you hope to see, hear, and feel from her in the first few minutes?

4. Which of the core principles—There's always a bridge; Curiosity is key; What you assume is what you get; Each individual is a culture; No strings attached—will be most important for Lynn to keep in mind in those first moments?

(To read the authors' responses to these questions, visit www.artof connecting.**net**.)

JOE AND THE NEW KID

Joe, fifty-eight years old, has worked in the corporate offices of a well-known company in the restaurant industry for twenty years. His friends tease him about being a clerk after all these years.

"Clerk Two!" he corrects them, smiling broadly.

He's a good-natured guy who looks like he's eaten a few too many of the hamburgers the company is famous for. Some of his friends are salesmen and managers, but most of them are as easygoing as he is; the most stressful time of his day is the fifteen minutes he spends in rush-hour traffic on the way to the bar for a beer with his buddies after work. His hairline has receded so far over the past decade that there's not enough left to comb.

Joe is in charge of the company's real estate records. When he started, it was a relatively simple job because there were only nine stores—that's what they call fast-food places these days—but after two decades of buying and selling properties, the company has accumulated enough documents to fill one floor of a warehouse. Joe is king of his domain; he prides himself on being able to find any piece of paper a vice president or director might need within four minutes.

But just this morning Joe got some alarming news from the woman who has been his boss for the last eight years. All the paper real estate records are going to be converted into electronic data over the next six months. And he's the one who will be converting them—under the watchful eyes of a new young hotshot. It turns out that, first of the month, he'll be part of a new information systems department reporting to a kid young enough to be his son.

He thought something was a little fishy yesterday when one of the VPs came through and introduced him to the new phenom, a kid who started out on the crew in one of the stores, then was promoted to store manager and then, within six months, moved up to district manager. Now it all made sense.

Jason Loveway, his boss told him. That's the kid's name. An IT expert. Joe doesn't remember a lot about him except that he had a bunch of gel in his hair, had earrings—in both ears—and was wearing black leather oxfords. And Joe wouldn't be surprised if there were a tattoo under the neck of his lime green shirt.

Joe was perfectly content with the job and the boss he had.

1. If you were Joe's coach, how might you use each of the core principles—There's always a bridge; Curiosity is key; What you assume is what you get; Each individual is a culture; No

strings attached—to help him connect with his new young boss?

2. What questions would you ask Joe to determine which of the pathways—Clarify your intention; Notice your own reactions; Search for similarities; Use cues; Experiment and adjust—will be most helpful in overcoming obstacles to connecting with Jason?

3. Step into third-person perspective—an outside observer—and give Jason advice about how he might connect with Joe in their first week together.

(To read the authors' responses to these questions, visit www.artof connecting.**net**.)

MICHELE AND THE DATA WONKS

Michele, now in her thirties, is a successful executive who has worked in pharmaceuticals since getting her MBA eight years ago. Michele's parents were activists in the sixties, and, when she was growing up, there were always interesting people gathered around the kitchen table. She loved spending time with them, discussing issues and challenging each other's values and beliefs.

Her big successes came in the marketing department. She enjoyed working with the creative types there; they batted ideas around, tried out marketing strategies on one another, and had a lot of fun.

Michele always looks like a million bucks. She goes to the best hair designer in town to get her cut and highlights, and she wears expensive, offbeat suits and heels.

Recently, the CEO promoted her, hoping her creativity might

give the process improvement group a shot of energy. The first project she took on was the accounts-receivable process. In her new role, she's dependent on a handful of people she calls "data wonks." They're the ones who supply her with the numbers she needs. So far, the work is getting done, but it's not very satisfying.

Michele, who is Jewish, is offended by the way the data group mixes religion and business. "In the break room," she says, "they talk about their mission work as if everyone has a mission, and they listen to a Christian radio station in the office." She thinks they ought to keep that kind of thing to themselves.

When Michele tries to throw out a dilemma or hypothetical situation, in the hope of stirring up an interesting conversation, she gets nowhere. "There's no answer to those dilemmas," she tells us, "but they act like there is one clear right answer—and that it can be found in the Bible. They believe homosexuality is a sin; I just think gays make a group more diverse and interesting."

She's sure they don't approve of the way she dresses. "They probably think my skirt is too short and my heels are too high. I could go to a power lunch in New York City dressed the way I am. The only place they could go in their Dockers and T-shirts might be the golf course."

Michele admits she hasn't really sought them out. She just knows it wouldn't be an interesting conversation. "I miss the smart people and the rowdy dialogues in the marketing department. I think I need to take a transfer or just hunker down and do the work I'm good at."

1. What are the key differences here?

2. Step into second-person perspective by looking at Michele through one of the data processor's eyes. What are your impressions of her from this perspective?

3. If you were helping her to clarify her intention in a way that would help her connect, what might you propose?

4. Michele has limited herself to two options for coping with her situation. What other options might she be missing?

5. If you view this scenario from third-person perspective, it's easy to see the ways in which Michele is building barriers. What are some of them?

6. If you were a coach working with Michele, what recommendations might you make to her?

(To read the authors' responses to these questions, visit www .artofconnecting.**net**.)

CHAPTER 8

LEARNING ACTIVITIES

If you are a leader in search of team-building or workshop activities that help people to close the diversity gap, this chapter is for you. We've collected seven activities that will help people understand the core principles and implement the pathways we've discussed in this book. Some of the topics are linked; they build on and refer to each other. Some can be used on their own. We've varied the activities: some can easily be adapted for e-learning applications; others can be run with large groups; some involve conversation in pairs; others get participants up on their feet. Each activity comes complete with objectives, group size, time requirements, materials requirements, and process.

ACTIVITY 4.
SPECTRUM OF PERSPECTIVES

This activity gets people on their feet and moving around. It is important to ease into it so that participants feel comfortable enough with one another to express opinions on controversial issues.

Objectives

1. To demonstrate diversity of opinion
2. To experiment with other perspectives
3. To encourage discussion and interaction
4. To understand other viewpoints about diversity issues

Group Size: 10 to 30

Time: 30 minutes

Materials: Spectrum of Perspectives (handout)

Process

1. Ask participants to form a line in the shape of a horseshoe or rainbow so that they can see one another.

2. Distribute the *Spectrum of Perspectives* handout.

3. For the first statement ("I've had lots of experience in dealing with many kinds of differences"), ask people to choose the number from 1 (Strongly Disagree) to 10 (Strongly Agree) that best represents their own level of experience. Explain that the line they're standing in represents a continuum. Designate one end of the line to represent "1" and the other to represent "10" and ask participants to find their place on the continuum. Once

everyone has found a place, ask which are the 1s, which the 2s, which the 3s, and so on. Point out the median—the exact middle—and what number it is on the continuum. Ask representatives from near both ends to explain why they disagree or agree. Make it clear that there is no right or wrong answer— that it's simply interesting to see and hear about different levels of experience. Ask someone near the middle to talk about his or her number/level of experience. Notice where the "clumps" form and ask people what they think/surmise about that.

4. For the second statement ("I believe teams are more successful when everyone is alike"), ask people to decide which number best represents their own beliefs. Then ask them to find their place on the continuum. Ask people near each end to explain why they agree or disagree. Ask someone near one end to move to a place near the other end. Ask that person to state an opinion in a convincing way representing the place on the continuum where he or she is now standing.

5. Continue through the statements, asking for perspectives and viewpoints, occasionally requesting that people shift to another place on the continuum.

SPECTRUM OF PERSPECTIVES
(HANDOUT)

1. I've had lots of experience in dealing with many kinds of differences.

   Strongly Disagree   Strongly Agree

   | 1 | 2 | 3 | 4 | 5 | 6 | 7 | 8 | 9 | 10 |

2. I believe teams are more successful when everyone is alike.

   Strongly Disagree   Strongly Agree

   | 1 | 2 | 3 | 4 | 5 | 6 | 7 | 8 | 9 | 10 |

3. I will do whatever it takes to overcome obstacles to connection.

   Strongly Disagree   Strongly Agree

   | 1 | 2 | 3 | 4 | 5 | 6 | 7 | 8 | 9 | 10 |

4. I am comfortable in ambiguous situations.

   Strongly Disagree   Strongly Agree

   | 1 | 2 | 3 | 4 | 5 | 6 | 7 | 8 | 9 | 10 |

—from Claire Raines and Lara Ewing, *The Art of Connecting* (New York: AMACOM, 2006).

ACTIVITY 2.
PRIMARY AND SECONDARY
ASPECTS OF DIVERSITY

In their book *Workforce America!* Marilyn Loden and Judy Rosener define two dimensions of diversity—primary and secondary. The primary aspects of diversity are the things about us that people can see just by looking at us (except for sexual orientation). They're aspects of ourselves that we were born with. The secondary aspects are things we have some control over and things that can change during our lives. They are also aspects of ourselves we can choose to reveal or not to reveal. This activity helps participants explore these aspects of diversity and understand that we are all similar and different in all kinds of ways.

Objectives

1. To identify some of the many ways we can be similar to and different from others
2. To clarify that every group has diversity and that each person is a unique culture

Group Size: 5 to 50
Time: 15 minutes
Materials: 2 easels, 2 flip charts, markers

Process

1. On one flip chart, list the primary aspects of diversity: age, race, ethnicity, physical qualities, gender, sexual orientation. On the other, list the secondary aspects: work background, geographical location, marital status, military experience, religious beliefs, education, parental status, income. (From Marilyn Loden

and Judy Rosener, *Workforce America!* (New York: McGraw-Hill, 1990). Used by permission of The McGraw-Hill Companies.)

2. Introduce the two lists to the group, and define primary and secondary aspects of diversity. Cite *Workforce America!* as the source for this information.

3. Explain that the list of secondary aspects isn't complete; it's just a sample of other ways we can differ. Ask for other differences that might go on the list (for example, Myers-Briggs type, political affiliation, Mac vs. PC, analytical vs. big picture, feelings vs. facts). Write additions on the flip chart.

4. Ask the group, "What are the implications of looking at differences in this way?" (Possible answers: "Everyone on a team or in a group has things in common"; "No matter how similar a group may seem, each is unique"; "Valuing diversity is important to all of us.")

ACTIVITY 3.
POINTS OF VIEW

Seeing situations from different vantage points can be helpful when we encounter obstacles to connecting, when our biases get in the way, when we're having difficulty understanding, or when emotions are running high. This activity gives participants an opportunity to experience the three points of view we described in chapter 4.

Objectives

1. To think more creatively about real-life interactions
2. To develop personal flexibility by becoming skilled at moving between perspectives
3. To improve your understanding of others

Group Size: 6 to 20
Time: 30 minutes
Materials: none

Process

1. Give a brief overview of the three points of view—first-, second-, and third-person perspectives—and explain the benefits of using them when connecting with those who are different. There is background information in chapter 4.

2. Ask participants to find a partner and to move their chairs so that they face each other. Ask each person to think of a recent interaction or encounter with a spouse, partner, friend, or coworker that was neutral or positive. Give participants a few minutes to choose the scenario they'll examine. Ask the pairs

to choose Partner A and Partner B. Partner B will begin by telling Partner A about the interaction, exaggerating *first-person perspective*. This will be the "it's-all-about-me" version of the story. Partner A's job is to listen and to coach if B shows even a trace of empathy for the spouse, partner, friend, or coworker. Partner A helps B to stay completely in first-person perspective. Allow about three minutes, and then switch roles.

3. For the next round, the partners trade chairs. Once again, begin with B. Now B tells A about the same interaction, this time from *second-person perspective*, the point of view of the spouse, partner, friend, or coworker. A's job is to keep B on track, completely in the other's perspective. Allow about three minutes, and then switch roles.

4. For the third round, the partners stand side-by-side looking at the chairs. Beginning with B's scenario, both partners imagine Partner B and his or her spouse, partner, friend, or coworker sitting in the chairs in the midst of the interaction. A and B are now in *third-person perspective*. They are outside observers coaching B. Their goal in this round is to observe new and original things they had not noticed before and discuss them with each other. Allow about three minutes, and then switch roles.

5. Bring the whole group together to debrief the activity. What was it like to be completely in first-person perspective? Second? Third? Which position was most difficult to stay in? Which offered the most insights? How might changing your perspective be valuable when interacting with someone who differs from you?

6. If time permits, repeat the process with a difficult, emotional, failed, or high-stakes interaction.

ACTIVITY 4.
CASE STUDY: CONVERGING NETWORKS

This whole-group activity works with a case study in unique ways that get participants on their feet and personally involved—in the challenge and in its solution.

Objectives

1. To examine the implications of finding similarities and noticing differences
2. To understand the ways loyalty can interfere with a process
3. To apply the core principles

Group Size: 20 to 40

Time: 1 hour

Materials: Converging Networks (handout), 2 easels, 2 flip charts, markers

Process

1. Distribute the *Converging Networks* handout. Ask for a volunteer to read it out loud as people follow along.

2. Ask people to look through the case study and decide which side they identify with more—the voice people or the data people. Make a clear boundary down the middle of the room. Ask the voice people to move to one side and the data people to the other. Then send one group into the hallway or into a nearby room. Each group will now spend about five minutes together going through the details of the case study to get clear on its own characteristics and the characteristics of the other group.

3. Bring the groups back together, maintaining the boundary between them. Ask the voice people what they think of the data people and the data people what they think of the voice people. This will probably involve lots of banter and fun. Record responses on the flip charts. Limit this to three or four minutes. Then ask the group, "Are you noticing more similarities or more differences?" Go through each response on the flip charts and put a D (difference) or S (similarity) beside it. (Most groups will have noticed primarily differences; we've set it up that way.) If most of the responses are differences, ask for some similarities. Record them on the flip chart. Ask, "What does this tell us about our tendencies if we are noticing mostly differences?"; "What are the implications when we notice similarities?"

4. Make a flip chart with the core principles:

   • There's always a bridge.
   • Curiosity is key.
   • What you assume is what you get.
   • Each individual is a culture.
   • No strings attached.

   Ask the group to now take on the role of organizational consultants who are facilitating the merging of voice and data. Then go through each of the core principles, asking questions like these:

   • (There's always a bridge.) "These two groups have common goals. What might some of them be?"; "How could you help them identify commonalities?"
   • (Curiosity is key.) "What is preventing these two groups from being curious and interested in each other?"; "What might be

done to remove those barriers?"; "How might you get them more interested and appreciative of each other?"

- (What you assume is what you get.) "What assumptions are the groups making about each other?"; "How will those assumptions affect the outcome of the merger?"; "How do you change someone's assumptions?"

- (Each individual is a culture.) "Are all voice people the same? All data people?"; "How has putting people into the two camps exacerbated the problem?"; "As organizational consultants, how might we depolarize this situation with the two camps?"

- (No strings attached.) "Which group is likely to have to change more? Why?"; "What kinds of reactions may that cause?"; "How can we help people to manage their expectations and understand that the merging of the two systems may be far more difficult for their group than the other?"

5. Ask, "In light of all we've talked about, what are some specific ideas you have for how to best implement this merger?" Record these on the flip chart. (Possible responses: "Have the merged group report to a [formerly] voice person rather than a data person"; "Set up small teams with representatives from both groups"; "Merge the groups slowly"; "Begin by setting high-level goals"; "Get representatives from both groups to design processes for the merger.")

CONVERGING NETWORKS
(HANDOUT)

Over the next few years, we'll be seeing more and more companies merging their voice systems and their data communications into one. Companies will eventually scrap their aging phone systems and route voice conversations over a network that includes applications like e-mail. Such projects are technically challenging. What sometimes proves even more difficult is getting the two sets of specialists to work together. Voice people and data people are different. They don't usually work together. Their personalities, communication styles, and work styles contrast. In most companies, there is a mutual lack of appreciation for what each contributes. And they distrust each other.

Voice workers tend to be older. In most companies, they're part of the facilities group, the people who fix the copy machines and the air conditioning. They are steadfast and reliable, and you can count on them in a crunch. They have regular direct contact with their customers. When the phones go down, they're expected to get things fixed on the double. The solutions they come up with aren't always beautiful; they'll use bailing wire and duct tape if that's what it takes to get things up and running again.

Data specialists are usually younger. They often report to the CIO, chief information officer, which puts them on an upper rung of the org chart. They are innovative and entrepreneurial, and they enjoy the challenge of thinking on their feet. Their relationship is with technology—the server. They're somewhat removed from customer demands, and they usually don't work under the same time pressure as the voice engineers. Data people pride themselves on technically elegant solutions to programming issues.

A common HR approach merges the two groups with everyone reporting to the CIO. But the voice people often aren't happy about giving up their turf, especially when their new boss is a data person who may not value their expertise and experience.

Successful network convergence will be essential to communication success for many companies in the next decade. But how will it all come together if the two teams are polarized and they're lobbing grenades over the wall at each other?

—from Claire Raines and Lara Ewing, *The Art of Connecting* (New York: AMACOM, 2006).

ACTIVITY 5.
CLARIFY YOUR INTENTION

Connecting across differences carries more risk of misinterpretation than communication with those similar to us. One way to minimize the risk is to specify what you hope to accomplish—your intention. This activity gives people an opportunity to think through a positive intention for a relationship they would like to improve.

Objectives

1. To practice clarifying intention
2. To show that clarifying your intention is effective in connecting across difference

Group Size: 10 to 30

Time: 30 minutes

Materials: Intention (handout), flip chart, markers

Process

1. Give a brief overview of what it means to *clarify your intention.* There is background reading in chapter 3. Give some examples of *intention* and write them on the flip chart.

2. Distribute the *Intention* handout. Ask participants to think of a relationship they would like to improve. Tell them they will not be asked to disclose this information. The relationship can be with a colleague, friend, or family member. It doesn't have to be a relationship that isn't going well—just one they would like to improve. Then ask people to take a few minutes to think through and write an answer to the first question ("What

is your long-term intention—for yourself and for the other person—for this relationship?"). Allow three or four minutes. Ask for volunteers to share the intentions they wrote.

3. Now ask participants to take a few minutes to think through and write an answer to the second question ("Think of a possible upcoming interaction you might have with the person. What might your intention for that interaction be—for yourself?—for the other?"). Allow three or four minutes. Ask for volunteers to share what they wrote.

4. Ask participants to complete the third set of questions ("In that interaction, how will you know if you're achieving your intention? How will you know if you're blowing it?"). Ask for volunteers to share what they wrote.

5. Debrief by asking questions such as these: "What is the benefit to deciding ahead of time what your intention is?"; "Why is this especially important when the other person is different from you?"

INTENTION
(HANDOUT)

Knowing what you want to accomplish ahead of time focuses your attention and guides your interactions in a constructive direction.

1. What is your long-term intention—for yourself and for the other person—for this relationship?

2. Think of a possible upcoming interaction you might have with the person. What might your intention for that interaction be—for yourself?—for the other?

3. In that interaction, how will you know if you're achieving your intention? How will you know if you're blowing it?

—from Claire Raines and Lara Ewing, *The Art of Connecting* (New York: AMACOM, 2006).

ACTIVITY 6.
THE TITANIUM RULE

Everyone has heard of the Golden Rule—do unto others as you would have them do unto you—and most people have heard of the Titanium Rule—do unto others according to their druthers—or something like it. But few people are skilled at using the Titanium Rule. This activity gives participants an opportunity to apply it in a fun group activity.

Objectives

1. To practice applying the Golden Rule and the Titanium Rule
2. To evaluate the effectiveness of each rule in connecting across difference

Group Size: Unlimited, but put people into groups of 5
Time: 20 to 30 minutes
Materials: Golden Rule/Titanium Rule (handout)

Process

1. Give a brief overview of The Golden Rule and The Titanium Rule. There is background information in chapter 1.

2. Divide participants into groups of 5. Distribute the *Golden Rule/Titanium Rule* handout. Talk through the scenario on the handout with the whole group. Then ask each group to brainstorm together and come up with as many ideas as they can in three minutes to the first set of questions (If you were following the *Golden Rule*—using your own natural style—how might you approach her? What kinds of things would you tell her about your company? How would you deliver your message?).

3. Now ask the groups to focus on the second set of questions (If you were following the *Titanium Rule*, how might you approach her? What kinds of things would you tell her about your company? How would you deliver your message?).

4. Bring the whole group back together. Ask for some examples of Golden Rule thinking and then for some examples of Titanium Rule thinking.

5. You may want to debrief the participants with some of these questions: "Which approach would be more likely to succeed with the woman at the party? Why?"; "Why is this concept important when we're dealing with people from other cultures?"; "Is the person in the scenario being phony by using the Titanium Rule?"; "Why is it challenging for most of us to incorporate the Titanium Rule into our everyday interactions?"

GOLDEN RULE/TITANIUM RULE (HANDOUT)

The Golden Rule: Do unto others as you would have them do unto you.

The Titanium Rule: Do unto others according to their druthers.

The Scenario

You are logical and orderly. You prefer not to be in the limelight. You like specifics, details, facts, and well-reasoned ideas. You are calm and rather quiet.

You are at a dinner party, and you meet someone whom you think would be a great addition to your company, even though she's very different from you.

She has circulated around to chat with every person at the party, and she seems to have found a personal connection with everyone. She leans in toward people, sometimes turns one ear toward them, and occasionally touches an arm or shoulder, as if what they're saying is important to her.

You decide to recruit her for your company.

Questions

1. If you were following the *Golden Rule*—using your own natural style—how might you approach her? What kinds of things would you tell her about your company? How would you deliver your message?

2. If you were following the *Titanium Rule*, how might you approach her? What kinds of things would you tell her about your company? How would you deliver your message?

—from Claire Raines and Lara Ewing, *The Art of Connecting* (New York: AMACOM, 2006).

ACTIVITY 7.
PRECLASS INTERVIEW

A few years ago, Nikki Moss developed a class called "Diversity for Leaders" for DTE Energy in Detroit. Before the start of the course, participants conduct an interview with someone of a race or ethnic group different from their own. In the first session, participants share the responses—not the names. We've adapted Nikki's interview activity so that it can be used to introduce the core principles and pathways.

Objectives

1. To promote learning and understanding of the experiences and beliefs of people from other races and cultures
2. To identify ways to be a supportive colleague
3. To identify principles and pathways for connecting across difference

Group Size: Works best with small groups of no more than about 16 people, where participants feel comfortable sharing the information they learned and their reactions to the interview.

Time: 1 hour for the interview; 1 hour in the session

Materials: Sample Introduction Letter, Interview Questions, *Principles and Pathways* (handout), 2 easels, 2 flip charts, markers.

Process

Two weeks before the session, send out the Introduction Letter and the Interview Questions. (Optional: two or three days before the session, call or e-mail participants to confirm that they have completed the interview and will bring their interview notes with them.)

1. Explain the purpose of the activity. Remind participants that the names of the people they interviewed are to be kept confidential.

2. Ask the group what the interview process was like for them. Record one- to two-word answers on the flip chart. Look for a variety of responses ("interesting," "awkward," "valuable," "uncomfortable," "fun"). Compliment the group members on noticing their reactions and paying attention to them. All of these thoughts and emotions are typical and expected when we're interacting with people who differ from us. Point out that it is important when we are seeking to connect across differences that we notice our own reactions. Sometimes our most limiting beliefs and attitudes live below the surface until they are provoked. When emotional triggers kick in, it's time to check what's going on inside us to determine whether our responses help or get in the way. Allow about ten minutes.

3. Ask if participants answered the questions for themselves before conducting the interview. Nikki Moss tells us that white Americans, for example, sometimes feel uncomfortable asking the interview questions of someone else because they're not proud of their own culture. She helps people to see there are all sorts of things to be proud of no matter what your background. Allow five to ten minutes.

4. Divide the group into pairs and give the pairs ten minutes to share the information they heard in their interviews. Then reunite the whole group and ask people to share some of the

more important things they learned. Allow another ten minutes for this discussion.

5. Prepare two flip charts. Label one *Principles (Values, Beliefs)* and the other *Pathways (Skills, Steps)*. Tell the group members you're going to focus now on the process of connecting with someone who differs from you—something they all were involved in when they conducted their interviews. For each, ask the group, "In your interviews, what values, beliefs, skills, and steps do you think contributed to connecting successfully?" Field as many answers as possible. Ask the group, "Is that more a principle or a pathway?" and then capture each response in a short phrase on the appropriate flip chart. Allow about fifteen minutes.

6. Distribute the *Principles and Pathways* handout. Explain each of the core principles and pathways briefly. (There is background reading in chapters 2 and 3.) Point out similarities between the responses on the flip chart and the handout. Allow about fifteen minutes.

SAMPLE INTRODUCTION LETTER

Dear Participant:

On (date), we will come together for (name of event) to work on becoming more effective at connecting with those who differ from us.

This effort is important to our organization for many reasons. Our workforce is becoming more and more diverse, and we need to tap into a variety of perspectives and approaches. Being the preferred employer, transferring knowledge, succession planning, recruiting, and retaining all require us to encourage a wide variety of backgrounds, viewpoints, and styles. Our customer base has become very diverse, and it's important that we continually improve our ability to connect with them so we don't miss opportunities and lag behind our competition.

For these reasons, I am asking you to conduct an employee interview before our first session with someone from another race, ethnic group, or culture. The purpose of the interview is to promote learning and understanding of the experiences and beliefs of people from other races and cultures and to identify ways to support them. When we get together, you will have an opportunity to share the responses—not the names—you receive to the interview questions and to talk about your interview experience.

Please conduct the interview in person, one-on-one, and in a relaxed setting—over coffee or lunch, perhaps, but not in your office. To begin the interview, explain its purpose and how the information will be used (anonymously, in a learning atmosphere). Put interviewees at ease and assure them that names and identities will be kept *in strict confidence*. Interviewees' names should not be written on your notes. If someone is uncomfortable answering any of the questions, he or she is free to opt out.

Bring your interview notes—without the name of the person you interview—on (date). We will use it in our session, and it will inform much of the work we do. You may want to start off by asking the interview questions of yourself.

I look forward to seeing you soon.

(Closing,

Your Name)

—from Claire Raines and Lara Ewing, *The Art of Connecting* (New York: AMACOM, 2006).

INTERVIEW QUESTIONS

1. What do you like about your ethnic group, race, or culture?

2. What do you wish other people understood or knew about your culture?

3. Do you feel all your work-related talents and skills are used on the job?

4. What challenges do you face at work that may have to do with your race, culture, or ethnicity?

5. How can I, as a colleague, support you?

—from Claire Raines and Lara Ewing, *The Art of Connecting* (New York: AMACOM, 2006).

PRINCIPLES AND PATHWAYS
(HANDOUT)

The Core Principles

- There's always a bridge.
- Curiosity is key.
- What you assume is what you get.
- Each individual is a culture.
- No strings attached.

Pathways

1. Clarify your intention.
2. Notice your own reactions.
3. Search for similarities.
4. Use cues.
5. Experiment and adjust.

—from Claire Raines and Lara Ewing, *The Art of Connecting* (New York: AMACOM, 2006).

ASSESSMENT

Take a moment to assess your current level of effectiveness at bridging the gap between you and people who differ from you. Ask yourself to what degree each of the ten statements below describes you. Assess yourself honestly; you've got nothing to lose and everything to gain.

1. I interact well with people from other backgrounds, and they give me positive feedback and are eager to meet with me again.

NEVER   RARELY   SOMETIMES   USUALLY   ALWAYS

2. I believe that, no matter how different we are, we can always find something in common, and I'm good at finding those commonalities.

NEVER   RARELY   SOMETIMES   USUALLY   ALWAYS

3. I'm genuinely interested in people who differ from me, and I'm able to communicate my interest to them.

NEVER   RARELY   SOMETIMES   USUALLY   ALWAYS

4. When I meet someone who is different from me, I assume I can learn interesting things from him or her.

NEVER   RARELY   SOMETIMES   USUALLY   ALWAYS

5. I approach each person as a unique individual instead of categorizing people as members of a certain group.

NEVER   RARELY   SOMETIMES   USUALLY   ALWAYS

6. I don't necessarily expect my interest in others to be returned. I know I'll get something from the interaction even if the other person doesn't show interest in me.

NEVER   RARELY   SOMETIMES   USUALLY   ALWAYS

7. In interactions with people of other races, ethnicities, religions, political beliefs, and generations and with people of other differences, I figure out what my goal is, what I want to accomplish, or how I want the other person to feel when the interaction is over.

NEVER   RARELY   SOMETIMES   USUALLY   ALWAYS

8. In such interactions, I tune in to my own reactions, thoughts, feelings, and hunches. When I notice that my reactions are getting in the way, I can shift to a more constructive approach.

NEVER   RARELY   SOMETIMES   USUALLY   ALWAYS

9. I am able to sense what others are thinking and feeling, and I'm able to respond effectively.

NEVER   RARELY   SOMETIMES   USUALLY   ALWAYS

10. If my words and actions aren't working, I try something else and notice its effectiveness. I continue to experiment until I get it right.

NEVER   RARELY   SOMETIMES   USUALLY   ALWAYS

SCORING

For each *Never*, give yourself 1 point.
For each *Rarely*, 2 points.

For each *Sometimes*, 3 points.
For each *Usually*, 4 points.
For each *Always*, 5 points.

If you scored between 10 and 19 points, you're uncommonly honest. If you want to change, it can be done. Begin immediately! Use everything you learned in this book and enroll in a workshop about diversity. Improving your attitudes and skills could make a big difference in your effectiveness.

If you scored between 20 and 29 points, your ability to connect with those who differ may be interfering with your effectiveness. Continue working on your skills.

If you scored between 30 and 39 points, you generally connect well with those who differ from you. Step out into third-person perspective now and then to evaluate your interactions and coach yourself on ways to be more effective based on what you've learned here.

If you scored between 40 and 49 points, you're excellent at connecting with those who differ from you. We hope you found lots of information here to help you become even more effective.

If you scored 50 points, Congratulations! We should have included you in chapter 1, "Masters of Connection."

NOTES

CHAPTER 1. MASTERS OF CONNECTION

1. Bill Kirtz, "Talk Radio That Means Something," *The Quill* (December 1997).
2. Terry Gross, *All I Did Was Ask* (New York: Hyperion, 2004).
3. Terry Gross, *Fresh Air* (radio broadcast on WHYY [National Public Radio], December 5, 2002).
4. Renee Montagne, "Interview: Terry Gross Discusses the 25th Anniversary of *Fresh Air*," *Morning Edition* (radio broadcast on National Public Radio, September 1, 2000).
5. Ibid.
6. Ibid.
7. Thomas Kunkel, "Interviewing the Interviewer," *American Journalism Review* (July 2001).
8. Anna Christopher, "What to Ask the Woman Who's Already Asked It All," *Programs A–Z* (radio broadcast on Vermont Public Radio, Fall 2004), available at www.vpr.net.
9. John Giuffo, "PW Turns the Tables on Terry Gross," *Publishers Weekly* (July 19, 2004).
10. Orville Schell, "Proving the Singular Value of a Voice in the Dark," The Year in Review: Television/Radio, *New York Times* (December 30, 2001).
11. Ibid.
12. Ibid.

CHAPTER 2. THE CORE PRINCIPLES

1. *Psychology Today* Staff, "Four Paths to a Happier You." *Psychology Today,* Jan./Feb. 2004

2. Learning Point Associates, "enGauge® 21st Century Skills: Literacy in the Digital Age," North Central Regional Educational Laboratory, www.ncrel.org/engauge/skills/skills.htm.

3. Richard F. Taflinger, "Taking Advantage," available at www.wsu .edu:8080/~taflinge/index.html.

4. Rupert Sheldrake, *Seven Experiments That Could Change the World* (New York: Riverhead Books, 1995).

5. James Rhem, "Pygmalion in the Classroom," *The National Teaching and Learning Forum* (Feb. 1999).

6. *The O'Reilly Factor* (October 9, 2003), Fox News Channel.

7. Bill O'Reilly, "Back of the Book: O'Reilly Discusses NPR Interview," *The America's Intelligence Wire* (September 21, 2004), Fox News Channel. Copyright 2004. Financial Times Information Ltd.

CHAPTER 3. PATHWAYS TO CONNECTION

1. John H. Kennedy, "Terry Gross Makes Conversation Seem Like a Breeze on 'Fresh Air,'" *Christian Science Monitor* (May 6, 1997).

2. Thomas Kunkel, "Interviewing the Interviewer," *American Journalism Review* (July 2001).

CHAPTER 5. WORKING WITH DIFFERENCES IN GROUPS

1. Jeffrey Mishlove, *Thinking Allowed: Conversations on the Leading Edge of Knowledge and Discovery* (Berkeley, CA, 1995–1999); available at www.thinking-allowed.com.

2. Don Maruska, *How Great Decisions Get Made* (New York: AMA-COM, 2004).

3. Yasuhiko Genku Kimura, "Alignment Beyond Agreement," *Journal for Integral Thinking for Visionary Action* 1, no. 4 (2003). Printed with permission of Vision in Action and Yasuhiko Genku Kimura. Essays by Mr. Kimura can be found at www.via-VisionInAction.org.

CHAPTER 6. TWENTY QUESTIONS

1. Donna J. Bear, "The Diversity/Innovation Link," *TrendWatcher* 276 (August 19, 2005).

2. Roger Axtell, *Gestures: The Do's and Taboos of Body Language Around the World* (New York: Wiley, 1991).

RELATED READING

Fisher, Roger, and Scott Brown. *Getting Together: Building Relationships as We Negotiate*. New York: Penguin, 1989.

Fisher, Roger, and Daniel Shapiro. *Beyond Reason: Using Emotions as You Negotiate*. New York: Viking Adult, 2005.

Fox, Jonathan. *Acts of Service: Spontaneity, Commitment, Tradition in the Nonscripted Theatre*. New Paltz, N.Y.: Tusitala Publishing, 2003.

Gross, Terry. *All I Did Was Ask: Conversations with Writers, Actors, Musicians, and Artists*. New York: Hyperion, 2004.

Heim, Pat, and Susan Golant. *Hardball for Women*. New York: Plume, 2005.

Heim, Pat, and Susan Golant. *Smashing the Glass Ceiling*. New York: Simon & Schuster, 1995.

Heim, Pat, and Susan Murphy. *In the Company of Women*. New York: Jeremy Tarcher, 2003.

Knight, Sue. *NLP at Work: The Difference That Makes a Difference in Business*. London and Naperville, Ill.: Nicholas Brealey, 1995.

Loden, Marilyn, and Judy Rosener. *Workforce America!* New York: McGraw Hill, 1990.

Maruska, Don. *How Great Decisions Get Made: 10 Easy Steps for Reaching Agreement on Even the Toughest Issues*. New York: AMACOM, 2003.

Raines, Claire. *Beyond Generation X: A Practical Guide for Managers*. Menlo Park, Calif.: Crisp Publications, 1997.

Raines, Claire. *Connecting Generations: The Sourcebook for a New Workplace*. Menlo Park, Calif.: Crisp Publications, 2003.

Raines, Claire, and Jim Hunt. *The Xers & the Boomers: From Adversaries to Allies*. Menlo Park, Calif.: Crisp Publications, 2000.

Salas, Jo. *Improvising Real Life: Personal Story in Playback Theatre*. New Paltz, N.Y.: Tusitala, 1999.

Steckel, Richard, and Michele. *The Milestones Project: Celebrating Childhood Around the World*. Berkeley, Calif.: Tricycle Press, 2004.

Zemke, Ron, Claire Raines, and Bob Filipczak. *Generations at Work: Managing the Clash of Veterans, Boomers, Xers, and Nexters in Your Workplace*. New York: AMACOM, 1999.

ABOUT THE AUTHORS

As a speaker, consultant, and workshop leader, Claire Raines helps people to understand the validity of other viewpoints. Her five books on the generations have sold more than 100,000 copies. *Generations at Work,* which she wrote with Ron Zemke and Bob Filipczak, was honored by Soundview as one of the top thirty business books of 2000. Claire has been featured widely in the media, including *CNN Financial News, Today, Business Week,* and *Fast Company.* She created the board game *Connecting Generations*™ and has hosted three training videos about generations in the workplace.

Claire and her husband, Allen, live in Denver and Fraser, Colorado. Avid travelers, devoted readers, mediocre tennis players, and decent fly fishermen, they have climbed eleven of Colorado's 14,000-foot peaks. For more information, visit www.generationsat work.com.

Lara Ewing has developed leaders throughout the world in performance and communication for thirty years. As a specialist in individual and team senior-leader effectiveness, Lara has worked in eighteen countries on five continents. Her corporate clients include nine Fortune 100 and fifteen Fortune 500 companies. Lara is the creator of the audio learning series *NLP Applications in Business* and co-creator of *Outrageous Consulting: 70 New Ways to Look at Your Situation.* She has appeared on *Good Morning Australia* and

Radio ABC. She particularly enjoys working with senior teams struggling to integrate widely differing points of view.

Lara is on the board of the Explorers Foundation, an organization dedicated to building a world fit for explorers. Visit www .explorersfoundation.org. She lives in the foothills of Colorado and in northern Mexico with her husband, Robert, and a beloved Briard, Leo. Her daughters, Shannon and Caitlin, have traveled the world with her since infancy. For more information, visit www .ewingandassociates.com.